BIBLE QUIZZES
& PUZZLES

CYRIL BARNES

TESTAMENT BOOKS

NEW YORK

This 2000 edition is published by Testament Books™,
an imprint of Random House Value Publishing, Inc.,
280 Park Avenue, New York, New York 10017,
by arrangement with Baker Book House.

Testament Books™ and design are trademarks of Random House Value Publishing, Inc.

Random House
New York • Toronto • London • Sydney • Auckland
http://www.randomhouse.com/

Previously published as Bible Quizzes & Puzzles, Volumes 1, 2, and 3

Printed and bound in the United States of America

8 7 6 5 4 3 2 1

1. CROSSWORD

ACROSS

1. Like grasshoppers and locusts (Nah. 3:15)
5. Exclamation
7. Can be free will or burnt
11. Negative
12. "To live is Christ and to . . . is gain" (Phil. 1:21)
13. "In your love you kept me from the . . . of destruction" (Isa. 38:17)
14. Double act
16. Discern
18. Father of Nahshon (1 Chron. 2:10)
20. Refusal
21. "I was a . . . and you invited me in" (Matt. 25:35)

DOWN

1. Night light
2. British driving side
3. Definite article
4. Generous do this freely (Ps. 37:26)
6. Employ
8. Where the brothers met Paul (Acts 28:15)
9. Rule
10. Son of Sheva (1 Chron. 2:49)
14. Son of Jacob (Gen. 30:6)
15. Leave out
16. They are worshiped in reverse
17. Father of Peleg q(1 Chron. 1:19)
19. Girl's name

2. MISSING WORDS

ADD the missing words and the puzzles will form a pattern.

A 1. "Each of us will give an . . . of himself to God" (Rom. 14:12)
 2. "Whoever . . . in the Son has eternal life" (John 3:36)
 3. "If you want to enter life, obey the . . ." (Matt. 19:17)
 4. "The Lord takes . . . in his people" (Ps. 149:4)
 5. "Do not be overcome by . . . but overcome . . . with good" (Rom. 12:21)
 6. "You are my . . . if you do what I command" (John 15:14)
 7. "No servant is . . . than his master" (John 13:16)
 8. "The leaves of the tree are for the . . . of the nations" (Rev. 22:2)
 9. "How shall we escape if we . . . such a great salvation?" (Heb. 2:3)
 10. "Don't grumble against each other, brothers, or you will be . . ." (James 5:9)

B 1. "The Lord is not slow in . . . his promise" (2 Peter 3:9)
 2. "Take my yoke upon you and. . . from me" (Matt. 11:29)
 3. "Preach this . . . : 'The kingdom of heaven is near'" (Matt. 10:7)
 4. "Love your . . . as yourself" (Matt. 19:19)
 5. "This is love: that we walk in . . . to his commands" (2 John 6)
 6. "Every good and . . . gift is from above" (James 1:17)
 7. "Many waters cannot . . . love" (Song of Songs 8:7)
 8. "In . . . and rest is your salvation" (Isa. 30:15)
 9. "It is God who arms me with . . ." (Ps. 18:32)
 10. "Where your . . . is, there your heart will be also" (Matt. 6:21)

3. BUNCHES OF DATES

A 1. When did Charles Wesley die? 1788, 1877, or 1689?
2. When did William Booth found The Salvation Army? 1856, 1865, or 1885?
3. When was the New English Bible (New Testament) first published? 1961, 1951, or 1971?
4. When did Francis of Assisi die? 1326, 1256, or 1226?
5. When was Augustine sent to convert the English? 697, 597, or 779?
6. When was John Wesley born? 1703, 1723, or 1733?
7. When did John Bunyan publish *Pilgrim's Progress*? 1678, 1687, or 1778?
8. When was Billy Graham born? 1910, 1912, or 1918?

B 1. When was the Authorized (King James) Version of the Bible first published? 1601, 1611, or 1621?
2. When was Martin Luther King, Jr. assassinated? 1966, 1968, or 1964?
3. When did Martin Luther appear before the Diet of Worms? 1511, 1521, or 1531?
4. When did John Milton publish *Paradise Lost*? 1657, 1667, or 1677?
5. When was Charles Spurgeon born? 1834, 1844, or 1854?
6. When was Thomas à Kempis converted? 1344, 1364, or 1374?
7. In which century did nobleman Bernard of Clairvaux live a secluded Christian life? 11th, 12th, or 13th?
8. When was Dietrich Bonhoeffer hanged? 1935, 1939, or 1945?

4. ALL IN THE AIR

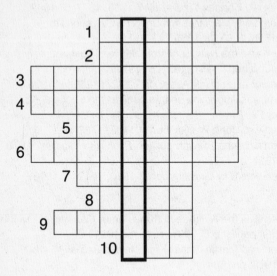

1. Noise in the sky
2. Always wet
3. Violent storm (Acts 27:14)
4. Elijah was caught up in one (2 Kings 2:1)
5. It came immediately with darkness (Acts 13:11)
6. Comes before thunder
7. A pillar guided the Israelites (Neh. 9:12)
8. Sins can become as white as this (Isa. 1:18)
9. Gentle wind
10. It stood still over Gibeon (Josh. 10:12–13)

Center column: The Lord hurled large ones down from the sky
(Josh. 10:11)

5. FIVE-LETTER WORDS

FILL in the squares according to the clues next to them. The last letter of the first line is the same as the first letter of the second line, and so on.

A

1
2
3
4
5
6
7
8
9
10

1. Brother of Moses (Exod. 4:14)
2. Not at all
3. Circles
4. Near Miletus (Acts 20:15)
5. In Psalms, possibly a musical term
6. Prophet (Hos. 1:1)
7. Place of sacrifice
8. Quick
9. Describes the smoke (Gen. 19:28)
10. A Harodite (2 Sam. 23:25)

B

1
2
3
4
5
6
7
8
9
10

1. One taken to another land
2. Hebrew measure (Num. 28:5)
3. Nothing sweeter (Judg. 14:18)
4. Works in bread
5. Complete
6. Rebekah's brother (Gen. 24:29)
7. After the day
8. Instruct
9. Caused by Paul (Acts 9:21)
10. Five do this to a hundred (Lev. 26:8)

Bible Quizzes & Puzzles

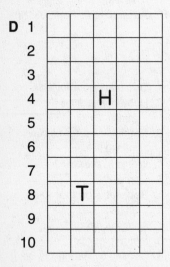

C

1.
2.
3.   O
4.
5.
6.   N
7.
8.
9.
10.

1. Day of plants and trees (Gen. 1:12–13)
2. Town near Lystra (Acts 16:1)
3. Home of a medium (1 Sam. 28:7)
4. Paul was a . . . citizen (Acts 22:25)
5. A prophet, an Elkoshite (Nah. 1:1)
6. May be thirty days
7. Needs to be blameless and upright (Ps. 119:7, 80)
8. Ties a sandal (Isa. 5:27)
9. River in Cush (Gen. 2:13)
10. Father of Jeroboam (1 Kings 11:26)

D

1.
2.
3.
4.   H
5.
6.
7.
8.   T
9.
10.

1. With peace and love (Jude 2)
2. Not old
3. They should lift up their heads (Ps. 24:7)
4. King of Heshbon (Deut. 2:24)
5. Hebrew month (Neh. 2:1)
6. Wife of Elimelech (Ruth 1:2)
7. Objects of worship
8. Pilfer or walk silently
9. Door fastener
10. King of Tyre (2 Sam. 5:11)

6. SIX FIVES

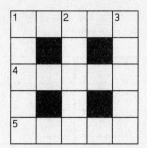

ACROSS

1. Later became Israel (Gen. 32:28)
4. Called the son of Pharaoh's daughter (Exod. 2:10)
5. People of Scotland

DOWN

1. Epistle writer
2. Universe
3. Public vehicles

7. INSTRUMENTS OF MUSIC

FILL in the missing letters and you will have the names of ten musical instruments mentioned in the Bible.

1. _ _ U _ P E _
2. _ Y _ E
3. _ I _ _ R _ M
4. _ A _ P
5. _ L _ T _
6. _ A _ _ O _ R _ _ E
7. _ _ M _ _ L
8. _ I _ H _ R
9. _ O _ N
10. _ I _ E

8. STUDIO FULL OF ART

EVERY answer contains the letters ART, which will appear down the central triple column.

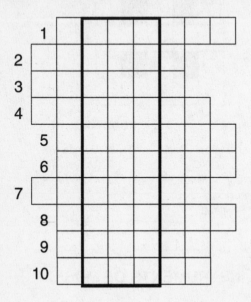

1. Like a bird to a snare (Prov. 7:23)
2. Four cubits high (Ezek. 43:15)
3. Shortage
4. Written rights
5. These gifts for Moresheth Gath (Mic. 1:14)
6. African pig
7. Israelites read the Book of the Law for this part of the day (Neh. 9:3)
8. Jesus spoke to Nicodemus of these things (John 3:12)
9. Stephen was the first (Acts 22:20)
10. Opened her home to Jesus (Luke 10:38)

9. A GOOD SCORE

ADD up the column for the final answer.

1. How many years before Paul "went up again to Jerusalem"? (Gal. 2:1) ....

2. For how many shekels was Joseph sold to the Ishmaelites? (Gen. 37:28) ....

3. Initially, how many donkeys did Job have? (Job 1:3) ....

4. How many miles from Emmaus to Jerusalem? (Luke 24:13) ....

5. How many shekels did Benjamin receive from Joseph? (Gen. 45:22) ....

6. How many years did it take to build the Jerusalem temple? (John 2:20) ....

7. How many disciples did Jesus send ahead? (Luke 10:1) ....

8. How many of David's men (besides Asahel) were missing after fighting Abner? (2 Sam. 2:30) ....

9. How many barley loaves did a boy give to Jesus? (John 6:8) ....

10. How many times was Peter willing to forgive? (Matt. 18:21) ....

11. How many virgins "went out to meet the bridegroom"? (Matt. 25:1) ....

Total: With the Lord, how many years are like a day? (2 Peter 3:8) ....

10. ALL MADE WELL

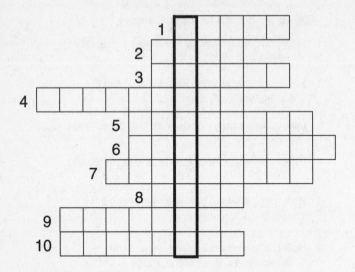

1. What sort of man was told to wash in the Pool of Siloam? (John 9:1, 9)
2. Where a widow's son was brought back to life (Luke 7:11–15)
3. A man suffering from . . . was healed in a Pharisee's house (Luke 14:2)
4. He was lowered on a mat to be healed (Luke 5:18–19)
5. A . . . woman was healed on the Sabbath (Luke 13:11–13)
6. What was the nationality of the one thankful leper who was healed? (Luke 17:16)
7. A . . . woman's daughter was cured of demon possession (Matt. 15:21, 28)
8. What sort of man heard Jesus say, "Ephphatha!"? (Mark 7:34–35)
9. Jesus healed his severed ear (John 18:10)
10. By what pool was a paralyzed man healed? (John 5:2)

Center column: Another blind man healed (Mark 10:46, 52)

11. ONE OF THREE

A 1. Who was a son of Noah? Dan, Ham, or On? (Gen. 5:32)
2. Who was the treasurer of the group of apostles? Judas, James, or Jannes? (John 13:29)
3. To whom did Jesus say, "Feed my sheep"? Peter, James, or John? (John 21:15)
4. Where did the city wall collapse in Joshua's day? Megiddo, Jericho, or Pimlico? (Heb. 11:30)
5. Where were followers of Jesus first called Christians? Athens, Antioch, or Attalia? (Acts 11:26)
6. Where did John write to "the seven churches"? Patmos, Patara, or Pathros? (Rev. 1:9)
7. Where did Simon the Leper live? Bethel, Bethany, or Bethsaida? (Mark 14:3)
8. Who was Queen of Ethiopia? Canaan, Candace, or Cana? (Acts 8:27)
9. What was the name of a proconsul of Achaia? Galilee, Gallio, or Galileo? (Acts 18:12)
10. Who was the secretary of King Jehoiakim's palace? Elijah, Elisha, or Elishama? (Jer. 36:12)

B 1. Where did Abraham plant a tamarisk tree? Beer Elim, Beeroth, or Beersheba? (Gen. 21:33)
2. Who was the great hymn-writer? Charles Kingsley, Charles Wesley, or Charles de Gaulle?
3. Who was the mighty preacher? Herbert Spencer, Edmund Spenser, or Charles Spurgeon?
4. Whose household informed Paul of arguments in the Corinthian church? Clara, Chloe, or Lydia? (1 Cor. 1:11)
5. Who wrote the "Hallelujah Chorus"? Hardie, Halley, or Handel?
6. Who became General of the Salvation Army in 1986? Eva Burrows, Eva Peron, or Eva Booth?
7. Who was the governor of Syria when Jesus was born? Quirinius, Augustur, or Tiberius? (Luke 2:2)
8. Who founded the Boy Scout Movement? Enoch Powell, Baden-Powell, or John Powys?

9. On which mountain did Elijah offer sacrifice? Carmel, Hermon, or Sinai? (1 Kings 18:20)
10. Where were the Israelites settled in Hoshea's day? Gaza, Gozan, or Gizon? (2 Kings 17:6)

C 1. From whose son did Jacob buy some land in Shechem? Haran, Hamor, or Hanan? (Gen. 33:19)
  2. Who founded the Church Army? Wilson Carlile, Thomas Carlyle, or Lewis Carroll?
  3. With which town was John Bunyan associated? Bedwas, Bedlington, or Bedford?
  4. Where was John Wesley born? Blisworth, Epworth, or Tamworth?
  5. Where was Albert Schweitzer born? Kayersberg, Nuremburg, or Hamburg?
  6. Whose ear did Peter cut off? Marcus, Malchus, or Micah? (John 18:10)
  7. Who replaced Judas Iscariot? Matthias, Mephistopheles, or Justus? (Acts 1:26)
  8. What was Naomi's name changed to? Mary, Mara, or Mala? (Ruth 1:20)
  9. The Israelites were subject to this King of Moab for eighteen years. Ehud, Elon, or Eglon? (Judg. 3:14)
  10. His estate was given to Queen Esther. Haman, Naaman, or Shalam? (Est. 8:1)

D 1. What is the name of a Jewish month? Adar, Adah, or Adam?
  2. Who was the first Baptist missionary to India? Andrew Carnegie, William Carey, or Howard Carter?
  3. Who was associated with Dwight Moody, the evangelist? Ira Sankey, Katherine Hankey, or Thomas Binney?
  4. Who was an outstanding convert in the days of Jesus? Mary of Bethany, Mary the mother of Jesus, or Mary Magdalene?
  5. Who is often spoken of as the doubting disciple? Peter, Bartholomew, or Thomas? (John 20:27)

6. Who was king of Tyre? Huram, Hiram, or Haram? (1 Kings 5:1)
7. From where did the Pilgrim Fathers sail for America? Tynemouth, Plymouth, or Teignmouth?
8. In what language was the Vulgate Bible written? French, German, or Latin?
9. Who was once a tax-collector? Matthew, Matthias, or Mattaniah? (Matt. 9:9)
10. Which prophet had a vision of red, brown, and white horses? Malachi, Haggai, or Zechariah? (Zech. 1:8)

12. CROSSWORD

ACROSS

1. Subjects of the Pharaoh (Gen. 12:14)
6. Small island
7. Civil order
11. Allow
12. Where the crowd flung dust (Acts 22:23)
13. Pronoun
14. Exclamation
15. Frozen water
17. The needy are lifted from this heap (Ps. 113:7)
19. King (French)
20. J____, brother of James (Jude 1:1)
22. Prayer must be without this (1 Tim. 2:8)

DOWN

1. Cried out
2. Father
3. On clocks and watches
4. Pronoun
5. "I have been anxiously ...for you" (Luke 2:48)
8. To exist
9. Town in the western foothills (Josh. 15:42)
10. Source of wool (Ezek. 27:18)
16. Indian language
18. King of Egypt (2 Kings 17:4)
20. Not down
21. And (French)

13. HIDDEN BIBLE LANDS AND ISLANDS

1. The coat was made with a fancy Prussian blue border.
2. The conversation was filled with dismal talk.
3. They found it a lying statement.
4. I love my Siamese cat.
5. We saw the face of Patsy riant and attractive.
6. To reach the capital of Russia we stop at Moscow.
7. The Swedes have made Malmo a beautiful city.
8. He had some dogs, just three, Gyp, Toby, and Nero.
9. Will Cedric retell his stories?
10. There is a spa in Leamington.

14. WHAT A JUMBLE!

A BIBLE MOUNTAINS

1. IARMBA
2. SOVILE
3. MARCEL
4. OILBAG
5. HIROAM
6. RBOAT
7. ZIMIGRE

B BIBLE JEWELS

All on the breastpiece in Exodus 28

1. LERBY
2. SPERJA
3. HINJACT
4. DREAMEL
5. PRISHAPE
6. THEMASTY
7. HEROCLISTY
8. UORIQUEST

15. BIBLE GROUPS

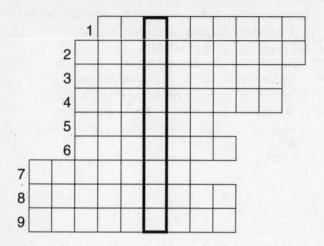

1. Samson was one of them (Judg. 13:5)
2. "Jews do not associate with . . ." (John 4:9)
3. They say "there is no resurrection" (Acts 23:8)
4. Plotted to kill Jesus (Mark 3:6)
5. Paul did this "straight at the Sanhedrin" (Acts 23:1)
6. Often associated with Pharisees (Luke 15:2)
7. Simon (not Peter) was one of them (Mark 3:18)
8. Revolutionary people (Luke 13:2)
9. Called "you hypocrites" by Jesus (Matt. 23:13)

Center column: Consecrated priests (2 Chron. 31:10)

16.   BIBLE BUILDINGS

1. At a special festival Israelites lived in these for seven days (Lev. 23:42)
2. Rahab's house was in this (Josh. 2:15)
3. The farmer wanted to tear them down to "build bigger ones" (Luke 12:18)
4. Protected defense for soldiers (2 Sam. 5:9)
5. We must remember those who live here (Heb. 13:3)
6. No room for Mary and Joseph here (Luke 2:7)
7. Will be left without occupants (Isa. 5:9)
8. Home for a king
9. Peter and John went here to pray (Acts 3:1)
10. Abram pitched these near Sodom (Gen 13:3)

Center column: Israelites' movable place of worship (Exod. 40:2)

17.   A CAGE OF JAYS

EACH name begins with "J" and the order of the second letter forms an interesting pattern.

1. One of Zebedee's sons (Matt. 10:2) ....
2. Madman driver (2 Kings 9:11) ....
3. Brother of Uz (Gen. 22:22) ....
4. Close friend of David (1 Sam. 19:1) ....
5. Traitor for thirty silver coins (Matt. 27:3) ....
6. Jesus raised his daughter to life (Matt. 5:23) ....
7. Father-in-law to Moses (Exod. 4:18) ....
8. Asher's eldest son (Gen. 46:17, AV) ....
9. Wore a "richly ornamented robe" (Gen. 37:3) ....
10. Epistle writer ....
11. Also called Israel (Gen. 32:28) ....
12. Prophet who claimed to be "only a child" (Jer. 1:6) ....
13. Son of Tola (1 Chron. 7:2, AV) ....
14. One in the desert, another on Patmos (Mark 1:4; Rev. 1:9) ....
15. Also called Barsabbas (Acts 1:23) ....

18. HARDLY A CLUE

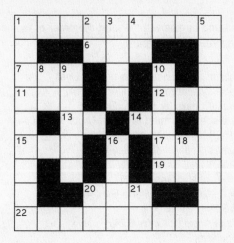

ACROSS

1. "May the God who gives . . . and encouragement give you a spirit of unity" (Rom. 15:5)
6. Jewish month (1 Kings 6:37)
22. Bible river (Gen. 2:14)

DOWN

1. Some wear these clothes (Luke 7:25)
5. "Do not do anything that . . . your neighbor's life" (Lev. 19:16)

Place these words in the spaces that are left after the outside words have been filled in.

AH   AIM   AM   APE   AV   BE   ERA   FAIR   IRA   LUG
MA   POT   RIOT   SIMLA   SOL   TABLE   UP   OR   UZ

19. A HIVE OF BEES

EACH name begins with "B" and the order of the second letter forms an interesting pattern.

1. Deborah asked him: "Has not the Lord gone ahead of you?" (Judg. 4:14) ....
2. Jacob left here for Haran (Gen. 28:10) ....
3. The place Paul "tried to enter" (Acts 16:7) ....
4. His girls gleaned the barley (Ruth 2:23) ....
5. Brother of Uz (Gen. 22:21) ....
6. "Set apart for me . . . and Saul" (Acts 13:2) ....
7. King of Aram (2 Kings 6:24) ....
8. A Shuhite (Job 2:11) ....
9. A cliff near Micmash (1 Sam. 14:4) ....
10. The month the Jerusalem temple was finished (1 Kings 6:38) ....
11. Jeremiah's scribe (Jer. 36:4) ....
12. Known for its Bible students (Acts 17:10) ....
13. Guarded the doorway at the king's gate (Esther 2:21) ....
14. Sons of Thunder (Mark 3:17) ....
15. Its young men "will fall by the sword" (Ezek. 30:17) ....

20. SIX IN THIRTY-SIX

REARRANGE the letters taking one at a time from each horizontal row to form the name of a person or place. For example, the first column will read NAAMAN.

A Old Testament men

1	2	3	4	5	6
N	J	E	D	J	H
O	L	A	O	A	A
N	S	G	I	S	A
E	G	I	M	H	J
A	A	A	U	P	E
A	L	H	I	H	N

1	2	3	4	5	6
N	J	E	D	J	H
A					
A					
M					
A					
N					

B Bible women

1	2	3	4	5	6
M	R	H	E	M	H
S	A	I	A	U	A
L	R	C	N	T	R
I	H	N	D	T	H
E	A	H	A	A	E
R	M	H	L	H	A

1	2	3	4	5	6
M	R	H	E	M	H

C Places in the Acts of the Apostles

1	2	3	4	5	6
L	A	P	T	C	R
H	Y	Y	A	T	A
P	R	H	O	S	P
R	D	S	H	T	E
O	R	N	U	E	U
S	S	S	A	S	S

1	2	3	4	5	6
L	A	P	T	C	R

D Old Testament towns

1	2	3	4	5	6
B	G	H	M	Z	G
I	I	E	I	I	E
B	Z	K	B	L	T
E	G	L	H	R	P
E	O	A	A	A	A
G	H	L	L	H	N

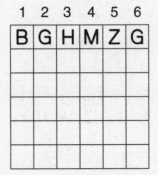

1	2	3	4	5	6
B	G	H	M	Z	G

E Men of the Gospels

1	2	3	4	5	6
A	P	T	S	J	J
O	N	A	H	I	H
O	M	S	I	D	I
E	M	R	A	E	L
I	O	P	A	U	E
W	S	S	P	H	N

1	2	3	4	5	6
A	P	T	S	J	J

F More Old Testament men

1	2	3	4	5	6
I	E	G	D	M	N
I	A	A	S	L	A
R	I	A	D	N	B
O	I	E	S	I	O
A	T	H	A	U	O
N	S	H	H	A	H

1	2	3	4	5	6
I	E	G	D	M	N

21. MOTHERS OF THE BIBLE

WHEN you have completed the answers you will find that the initial letters spell the name of the king who was Naamah's son.

1. Mother of Jacob (Gen. 27:5)   ....
2. Mother of Timothy (2 Tim. 1:5)   ....
3. Mother of Samuel (1 Sam. 1:20)   ....
4. Ruth was the mother of . . . (Matt. 1:5)   ....
5. Mother of Solomon (1 Kings 2:13)   ....
6. Mother of Korah (Gen. 36:5)   ....
7. Mother of Ahaziah (2 Kings 11:1)   ....
8. Mother of Jesus (Matt. 1:18)   ....

22. BIBLE LANDS

IF you supply the missing letters you will have the names of ten Bible lands.

1. _ A _ A R _ A
2. _ _ H _ O P _ A
3. _ I _ Y _
4. _ P _ _ N _
5. _ S _ Y _ I A
6. _ E R _ I _
7. A _ _ B _ A
8. _ E S _ _ O T _ M _ A
9. _ H _ E N _ C I _
10. _ S R _ _ L

23. AN ODD ONE OUT

ONE word in each list does not fit into the pattern.

A 1. Romans, Jude, Psalms
2. Good News, Book of
   Common Prayer, Moffatt
3. Aaron, Naphtali, Asher
4. Euphrates, Tigris, Tiber
5. Faith, hope, kindness
6. Aramaic, Greek, Coptic
7. Shem, Ham, Joseph
8. Onyx, diamond, beryl
9. Snowdon, Ararat, Gilboa
10. Dollar, penny, shekel

B 1. Spain, Italy, Portugal
2. Mauve, yellow, red
3. Sword, gun, arrow
4. Cloak, coat, guernsey
5. Pergamum, Rome,
   Philadelphia
6. Oak, sycamore, maple
7. Piano, harp, trumpet
8. Pharaoh, sultan, Caesar
9. Peter, Jonah, Isaiah
10. Baboon, buffalo,
    antelope

24. HIDDEN BIBLE FLOWERS AND PLANTS

1. He is an ardent Christian worker
2. He drove the car away down the road
3. The tank was full of scum mingled with weeds
4. We find the gigantic roc usually in Eastern stories
5. He visited the farm and raked the soil
6. His journey was to and fro Seleucia
7. It proved to be an alkali lying on the bench
8. His halo escaped my view
9. He took panic as Siamese cats appeared
10. Good and ill winds often blow

25. CROSSWORD

	1	2	3		4	5	6	
	7				8			
9				10		11		12
13			14		15		16	
		17			18			
19			20				21	
22		23				24		
	25		26		27			
	28							

ACROSS

1. Prophetess (Judg. 4:4)
7. Avenue (abbrev.)
8. Weep
9. Be in debt
11. Servant of Solomon (Ezra 2:57)
13. Indefinite article
14. Merry month
16. Negative
17. Georgia
18. And (French)
19. Horsepower (abbrev.)
20. Heavy weight
21. Endless cereal _ _ (t)
22. Help!
24. Owns
25. Chemist
27. "Birds of the . . ."
28. Home of kings

DOWN

1. Daybreak
2. First woman
3. Exist
4. Roman Catholic
5. Son of Jether (1 Chron. 7:38)
6. Song
9. Take your . . . in his name (Deut. 6:13)
10. For motorists
12. Immeasurable amounts
14. Rug
15. Japanese coin
21. Disciples strained at them (Mark 6:48)
23. Spring
24. Go quickly
26. Savings and Loan (abbrev.)
27. Electric current

26. IN ALL DIRECTIONS

THE words appear forward, backward, upward, downward or diagonally. Circle each word.

A TEN NEW TESTAMENT BOOKS

```
M   A   R   K   N   C   G   Q
J   A   M   E   S   H   P   Y
S   U   T   I   T   E   O   H
L   A   C   T   S   B   Q   J
Z   W   Y   L   H   R   A   O
P   J   J   U   D   E   H   M
G   I   C   K   D   W   W   I
P   E   T   E   R   S   F   T
```

B THIRTEEN VERBS IN 1 CORINTHIANS 13:4–13

```
X   A   W   O   N   K   Q   K
Z   H   B   A   Y   V   N   E
C   O   M   E   S   D   F   E
F   P   U   T   B   O   G   P
R   E   J   O   I   C   E   S
K   S   T   S   U   R   T   M
I   D   E   K   L   A   T   H
K   D   R   E   M   A   I   N
```

C TWELVE OLD TESTAMENT BOOKS

```
N A H U M Z K A
U I H C A L A M
M J C G E E H H
B O J U S O M A
E N M D S J R I
R A F E J Z M A
S H A N E O P S
X Y H A G G A I
```

D THIRTEEN NOUNS IN PSALM 23

```
S E R U T S A P
T H B D O C Q A
A T E U U O W T
F A L P D C A H
F E K L H A T S
J D V H I E E F
A O T I D O R H
S T A B L E S D
```

27. SONGS OF PRAISE

SUPPLY the missing words from popular hymns.

1. Praise, my . . . , the King of Heaven
2. All praise to thee, my God, this . . .
3. Praise God, from whom all . . . flow
4. Fill thou my . . . , O Lord my God, In every part with praise
5. Praise to the Lord, the . . . the King of creation
6. Praise him! Praise himl Jesus, our . . . redeemer
7. All people that on earth do dwell, Sing to the Lord with cheerful voice; Him serve with mirth, his praise . . .
8. We praise thee, O God, our . . .
9. O for a . . . tongues to sing My great redeemer's praise
10. Let us with a . . . mind praise the Lord, for he is kind

28. BROKEN NAMES

A Take two groups of letters at a time, join them together, and you will have the names of ten Bible rivers.

NA   ABA   ON   HON
     ON   NI   GI
HA   KISH   RIS
          JOR   DAN
TIG   LE   PAR   PHAR
       BAR
PISH   BOR   KE

B As above, but in groups of two or three and you will have the names of ten minor prophets.

NA HAR AC ZEC HO JON

HAG OS IAH UK GAI IAH

AM JO SEA HAB AH HUM

HI AKK EL MAL HAN ZEP

29. SIX SEVENS

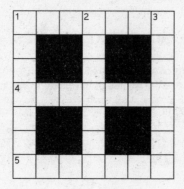

ACROSS

1. ". . . has broken"
4. Palace administrator (Isa. 37:2)
5. In your clothes under the south wind (Job 37:17)

DOWN

1. Trophimus was left here (2 Tim. 4:20)
2. Home of Canaanites (Judg. 1:30)
3. A set of rules for making sentences in a language

30. ON THE ROAD

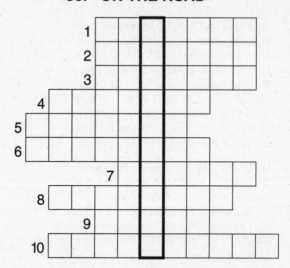

1. Israel was "carried into exile" on the road to this city (Matt. 1:17)
2. Philip sat in this on the Gaza Road (Acts 8:30)
3. A Levite and a Samaritan traveled on the road between here and Jerusalem (Luke 10:30)
4. Paul passed through this region and Phrygia (Acts 18:23)
5. Some Israelites were captured on this road (Num. 21:1)
6. Joram called for one (2 Kings 9:17)
7. Who was buried on the road to Bethlehem? (Gen. 35:19)
8. A general user of the road
9. These ways will be made smooth (Luke 3:5)
10. "Stand" here and "look" (Jer. 6:16)

Center column: A blind man sat by the wayside

31. WHO (OR WHAT) ARE WE?

A My first is in ABRAHAM but never in PAUL
My second's in HEARING but not found in CALL
My third's not in YOUNGISH but clearly in OLD
My fourth comes in FEARFUL but never in BOLD
My next misses ADAM but is part of EVE
My sixth shows in MERCY but not in DECEIVE
My next is in EVIL but never in GOOD
My last is in SILVER but never in WOOD
My whole is a name of the Lord Jesus

B My first is in ROD but never in STAFF
My next is in WIND but not in the CHAFF
My third's not in MOON but shining in SUN
My fourth is in CLOSING but not in BEGUN
My next is in MILKING but never in CREAM
My sixth's found in PASTURE but not in the STREAM
My seventh's in HOLDING and also in YIELD
My last's not in SOWING but firm in the FIELD
My whole is a follower of the Lord Jesus

C My first is in CANA and also in NAIN
My next's not in COMFORT but clearly in PAIN
My third is in GAZA and in ZION too
My fourth's not in PETER but there in ANDREW
In RAMAH's my fifth, though in GEBA left out
Next in EBENEZER, of this there's no doubt
No seventh in WINDOW but there in the GATE
My eighth's not in LOVING but seen well in HATE
My whole is the home of the Lord Jesus

D My first's not in CAMELS but part of the SHEEP
My second's in WHEAT, not in WEEDS by the heap
My third's seen in FLOUR but not in the YEAST
Though not in the MOST my next's in the LEAST
My fifth's not in GOOD fish but seen in the BAD
My sixth comes in LOST coin as well in the LAD
It misses SAMARITAN but seventh's in JEW
My last's in the MASSES but not in the FEW
My whole are stories the Lord Jesus told

32. CROSSWORD

ACROSS

1. They lived in Jerusalem (Josh. 15:63)
6. "The name of the wicked will . . ." (Prov. 10:7)
7. Not wet
11. Antelope
12. Surrounds the earth
13. Knockout
14. Not them
15. Nigerian language
17. Word of rebuke
19. Mineral spring
20. Single
22. Christ must have this in everything (Col. 1:18)

DOWN

1. They flashed like lightning (Hos. 6:5)
2. Home of Abraham (Gen. 11:31)
3. For washing hands
4. Pronoun
5. Shebna's office (Isa. 36:3)
8. Royal Navy
9. Territory in Canada
10. Endures
16. Could hold ice cream
18. Not down
20. Gold or yellow (heraldic color)
21. Printer's measure

33. HIDDEN BIBLE GEMS AND METALS

1. Good men can be seen growing old with gracefulness
2. There was never an emir on the throne of Israel
3. Hilkiah was a temple administrator for King Josiah
4. A sore tonsil very quickly inflames
5. We should do our best in all our work
6. Caleb, Ron, Zebedee, and Adam never met each other
7. Early Methodists found Mow Cop perfect for prayer meetings
8. When people in Babylon made a stop a zither was heard
9. Rub yellow and blue together for green
10. Beautiful is a gate in Jerusalem

34. ONE TO NINE

ADD the missing word in each sentence
1. "ONE . . . . I do know. I was blind but now I see" (John 9:25)
2. "The man with TWO . . . . should share with him who has none" (Luke 3:11)
3. "Let us put up THREE . . . . —one for you, one for Moses and one for Elijah" (Luke 9:33)
4. "A river watering the garden flowed from Eden, from there it was separated into FOUR . . . ." (Gen. 2:10)
5. "Are not FIVE . . . . sold for two pennies?" (Luke 12:6)
6. "There are SIX . . . . for work" (Luke 13:14)
7. "I tell you (forgive), not SEVEN . . . . but seventy-seven times" (Matt. 18:22)
8. "He (Moses) gave four carts and EIGHT . . . . to the Merarites" (Num. 7:8)
9. "Were not all ten . . . . ? Where are the other NINE?" (Luke 17:17)

35. CHANGING LETTERS

CHANGE one letter at a time to find a connected word.

A S O I L
_ _ _ _ baffle or beat off
_ _ _ _ "my covenant with him will never. . . ." (Ps. 89:28)
_ _ _ _ thin Scottish cake
_ _ _ _ place of crops and animals

B M E A T
_ _ _ _ surrounds a castle
_ _ _ _ raise a question
_ _ _ _ state of mind
_ _ _ _ Joseph's brothers came to buy this (Gen. 42:7)

C H E A T
_ _ _ _ "no place to lay his . . ." (Matt. 8:20)
_ _ _ _ "we were . . . prisoners" (Gal. 3:23)
_ _ _ _ ". . . on to the good" (1 Thess. 5:21)
_ _ _ _ "lukewarm—neither hot nor . . ." (Rev. 3:16)

D M A K E
_ _ _ _ "I do all this for the . . . of the gospel" (1 Cor. 9:23)
_ _ _ _ where goods change hands
_ _ _ _ fish or part of a foot
_ _ _ _ young ruler should have done this to everything
      he had (Luke 18:22)

36. ANOTHER GOOD SCORE

ADD up the column for the final answer.

1. The second debtor owed these bushels of wheat
   (Luke 16:7)   ....
2. How many disciples of Jesus saw Elijah and Moses?
   (Matt. 17:3)   ....
3. How many silver pans did the exiles bring back from
   Babylon? (Ezra 1:9)   ....
4. How long (months) did David live in Philistine
   territory? (1 Sam. 27:7)   ....
5. In Noah's day it rained . . . days and nights (Gen. 7:17)   ....
6. How many sheep were left on the hills in the parable
   of the lost sheep? (Luke 15:4)   ....
7. How many foxes did Samson catch? (Judg. 15:4)   ....
8. How many years was Aeneas bedridden? (Acts 9:33)   ....
9. How many times was Paul lashed by the Jews? (2
   Cor. 11:24)   ....
10. How many soldiers accompanied Paul on his journey
    to Caesarea? (Acts 23:23)   ....

Total: How many able men of the Hebronites were in
          David's service? (1 Chron. 26:30)   ....

37. SOMETHING OLD

EACH answer contains the letters OLD and appears in
alphabetical order of the initial letter.

1. "Speak your word with great . . ." (Acts 4:29)
2. Neither this nor hot (Rev. 3:15)
3. The shroud does this to all peoples (Isa. 25:7)
4. The fool does this with his hands (Eccles. 4:5)
5. They worked near the Sheep Gate in Jerusalem (Neh. 3:8)
6. " . . . on to faith and a good conscience" (1 Tim. 1:19)
7. Having many forms

8. The most ancient
9. A good fighter for Jesus Christ (2 Tim. 2:3)
10. Informed
11. "Do not . . . your mercy from me, O Lord" (Ps. 40:11)

38. NEIGHBORING KINGS

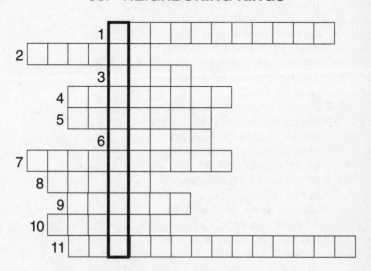

1. King of Assyria who attacked Hoshea (2 Kings 17:3)
2. King of Aram anointed by Elijah (1 Kings 19:15)
3. King of Egypt in Josiah's day (2 Kings 23:29)
4. King of Aram who besieged Samaria (1 Kings 20:1)
5. Title of Egyptian kings
6. King of Persia (2 Chron. 36:22)
7. King of Assyria (Ezra 4:2)
8. One of the cities where Og reigned (Josh. 12:4)
9. Assyrian king who captured Ashdod (Isa. 20:1)
10. He appointed Daniel an administrator (Dan. 6:1–2)
11. King of Babylon in Jehoiakim's time (2 Kings 24:1)

Center column: Another king of Assyria (2 Kings 18:13)

39. PUT ME RIGHT

CORRECT the wrong word in each verse.

1. Blessed is the man who does not talk in the counsel of the wicked (Ps. 1:1) ....

2. He feeds me beside quiet waters (Ps. 23:2) ....

3. God is might; in him there is no darkness at all (1 John 1:5) ....

4. Blessed are the sure in heart, for they will see God (Matt. 5:8) ....

5. Hate what is vile; cling to what is good (Rom. 12:9) ....

6. Put on the full armor of God so that you can make your stand against the devil's schemes (Eph. 6:11) ....

7. Do nothing out of selfless ambition or vain conceit (Phil. 2:3) ....

8. If we are faithful, he will remain faithful (2 Tim. 2:13) ....

9. Obey your readers and submit to their authority (Heb. 13:17) ....

10. If you love me, you will obey what I demand (John 14:15) ....

40. CROSSWORD

1		2	3		4	5	6	■
	■	7		■	8			9
10	11			■	12			
13		■	14			■	15	
16			■	■		17		
18		■	19	20		■	21	
22		23		■	24	25		
26				■	27		■	
■	28							

ACROSS

1. Reaps
7. That is
8. . . . and every
10. With a clock in prison
12. Through (abbrev.)
13. Preposition
14. Groove
15. Illinois (abbrev.)
16. Writing fluid
17. Where (Latin)
18. Seventh scale tone
19. Not cold
21. Prefix or suffix
22. Where they saw the star (Matt. 2:2)
24. Part of a church
26. Comes in flakes
27. Exist
28. The Lord's are trustworthy (Ps. 19:7)

DOWN

1. Linked with the Perizzites (Judg. 3:5)
2. Outer ring
3. Change direction
4. Long seat without end
5. Head covering in reverse
6. . . . and Pharisees
9. The Lord is "majestic in" (Exod. 15:11)
11. People of a Greek island
19. Melt ice and mix it
20. Could be taboo
23. Drunkard
25. Could you make this of the leviathan? (Job 41:5)

41. THEY ATE IT ALL

EVERY answer contains the letters ATE.

1. To kill
2. A fruit
3. Every other time
4. The best of all (1 Cor. 13:13)
5. With thankfulness
6. A man was standing here (Ezek. 40:3)
7. A tableland
8. Holy bread (Heb. 9:2)
9. As directed (2 Kings 6:10)
10. What God had made (Gen. 1:1)

42. BIBLE TOOLS

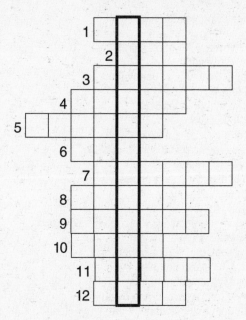

1. "Unless I see the . . . marks" (John 20:25)
2. Swung to fell a tree (2 Kings 6:5)
3. Breaks a rock to pieces (Jer. 23:29)
4. For shaking grain (Amos 9:9)
5. To spread out "fodder and mash" (Isa. 30:24)
6. "Hills once cultivated by the . . ." (Isa. 7:25)
7. For reaping (Jer. 50:16)
8. Used by a scribe (Jer. 36:23)
9. Not heard at the temple site (1 Kings 6:7)
10. "No one who puts his hand to the . . ." (Luke 9:62)
11. Used to pick up a live coal (Isa. 6:6)
12. Three-pronged one used at a sacrifice (1 Sam. 2:13)

The center column forms an interesting order of letters

43. OLD ENGLISH HYMNS

SUPPLY the missing words.

A 1. Dear Lord and . . . . . . of mankind
2. Rock of . . . . . . cleft for me
3. Guide me, O thou . . . . . . Jehovah
4. O Jesus, I have . . . . . .
5. Saviour, like a . . . . . . lead us
6. In . . . . . . love abiding
7. The sands of . . . . . . are sinking
8. Will your . . . . . . hold in the storms of life
9. Lo in the . . . . . . he lay
10. The strife is o'er, the . . . . . . done
11. I will sing the . . . . . . story
12. Now the day is . . . . . .

B 1. This is my father's . . . . . .
2. Praise, my soul, the . . . . . . of heaven
3. All things . . . . . . and beautiful
4. Once in . . . . . . David's city
5. Rescue the . . . . . . care for the dying
6. Go, labour on; . . . . . . and be spent
7. Let us with a . . . . . . mind
8. Away in a manger, no . . . . . . for a bed
9. It came upon the . . . . . . clear

44. SPELL A NAME

REARRANGE the letters in each row so that they spell a word; then the center column read downward will give you a Bible name.

A

E	M	L	A	P
N	E	A	L	C
	T	E	A	
	E	N	T	
	N	U	R	

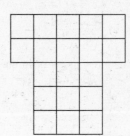

Center column: An apostle

B

E	R	T	H	O
T	C	H	O	L
	H	A	S	
	N	M	E	
	T	R	A	

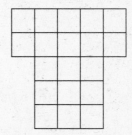

Center column: A prophet

C

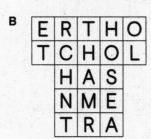

T	T	E	S	S
M	Y	E	T	P
	A	M	H	
	I	N	T	
	N	Y	A	

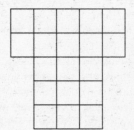

Center column: A European country
Center column: An explorer in Canaan

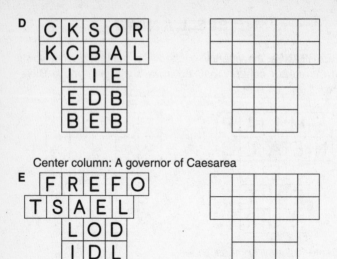

D

C	K	S	O	R
K	C	B	A	L
	L	I	E	
	E	D	B	
	B	E	B	

Center column: A governor of Caesarea

E

F	R	E	F	O
T	S	A	E	L
	L	O	D	
	I	D	L	
	X	E	A	

45. PUT ME RIGHT AGAIN

CORRECT the wrong word in each verse.

1. Placid are the meek, for they will inherit the earth (Matt. 5:5)
2. Bless those who prosecute you; bless and do not curse
   (Rom. 12:14)
3. You made him (man) a little higher than the heavenly beings
   (Ps. 8:25)
4. Lift up your hand, O God! Do not forget the hopeless (Ps. 10:12)
5. I have never seen the righteous forgiven (Ps. 8:25)
6. Let the wise listen and add to their leaning (Prov. 1:5)
7. He is able to deal gently with those who are ignoble (Heb. 5:2)
8. I give you this charm: Preach the Word! (2 Tim. 4:1)
9. My soul plans for you, O God (Ps. 42:1)
10. He was opposed and afflicted (Isa. 53:7)

46. CROSSWORD

|1| |2|3| |4|5| |█|
|—|—|—|—|—|—|—|—|—|
|█| |6| |█|7| |█|8|
9	10			11			12	
13			█		█	14		
█			15				█	█
16		17		█		18		19
20			21		22			
		23		█	24		█	█
█	25							

ACROSS

1. "A man of . . . heart does not prosper" (Prov. 17:20)
6. Joshua held his javelin toward this place (Josh. 8:18)
7. Pronoun
9. Describes the Lord's love (Ps. 13:5)
13. Violin string
14. Old cloth
15. Lightning lights it up (Luke 17:24)
16. Not hers
18. Emperor or empress (abbrev.)
20. "Come over to . . . and help us" (Acts 16:9)
23. H____, a garden tool (Isa. 7:25)
24. Without (abbrev.)
25. "The LORD is my . . . and my song" (Ps. 118:14)

DOWN

1. Stop a hole
2. One is used to float on the sea (2 Chron. 2:16)
3. By way of
4. Endless wave
5. Set in motion
8. A scorpion is never given in place of this (Luke 11:12)
10. African desert area
11. Marked with ink
12. She returned from Moab (Ruth 1:6)
16. Her majesty's ship (abbrev.)
17. Resident of Scotland
18. Gone backwards
19. Lead me in a straight one (Ps. 27:11)
21. Ever
22. Possess

47. MORE MISSING WORDS

ADD the missing words and the puzzles will form a pattern.

A 1. "He (Jesus) is the . . . . sacrifice for our sins" (1 John 2:2)
 2. (The Lord) "richly . . . . all who call on him" (Rom. 10:12)
 3. "Be . . . . to do what is right in the eyes of everybody" (Rom. 12:7)
 4. "Follow the way of love and eagerly . . . . spiritual gifts" (1Cor. 14:1)
 5. "Be . . . . O Lord, in your strength" (Ps. 21:13)
 6. "The righteous will live by . . . . " (Rom. 1:17)
 7. "May God be . . . . to us and bless us" (Ps. 67:1)
 8. " . . . . your father and your mother" (Exod. 20:12)
 9. "At evening let not your hands . . . . " (Eccles. 11:6)
 10. "Come before him with . . . . songs" (Ps. 100:2)
 11. "Consider therefore the . . . . and sternness of God" (Rom. 11:22)
 12. "Keep on . . . . each other as brothers" (Heb. 13:1)

B 1. The Lord "has done . . . . things" (Ps. 98:1)
 2. "God will meet all your . . . . " (Phil. 4:19)
 3. "We must . . . . God rather than men" (Acts 5:29)
 4. God will " . . . . us from all unrighteousness" (1 John 1:9)
 5. "The Lord's servant must not . . . . " (2 Tim. 2:24)
 6. "He who sows . . . . reaps a sure reward" (Prov. 11:18)
 7. "He (God) alone is my rock and my . . . . " (Ps. 62:2)
 8. " . . . . in the Lord with all your heart" (Prov. 3:5)
 9. "Thanks to the Lord for his . . . . love" (Ps. 107:15)
 10. "He gives us the . . . . through our Lord Jesus Christ" (1 Cor. 15:57)
 11. "God chose the . . . . things of the world to shame the strong" (1 Cor. 1:27)
 12. "Never be lacking in . . . . " (Rom. 12:11)

48. JUMBLED KINGS OF ISRAEL AND JUDAH

1. OJAMROBE
2. MOREAJH
3. LOMOONS
4. SOHEHA
5. IECHOINAJH

6. AHAZCHAIR
7. HIHAKEPA
8. MOREAHOB
9. HEHHOSTAJAP
10. SEANSHAM

49. THREE-LETTER CROSSWORDS

A

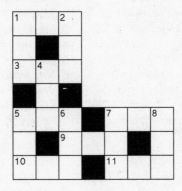

ACROSS

1. Mown grass
3. Drink
5. Honest measure (Lev. 19:36)
7. Help!
9. Paired with terebinth (Isa. 6:13)
10. Pits in Siddim (Gen. 14:10)
11. Tree

DOWN

1. Not cold
2. Old yes
4. Son of Benjamin (Gen. 46:21)
5. Head cover
6. Neither
7. "God called the expanse . . ." (Gen. 1:8)
8. ". . . magic charms on all their wrists" (Ezek. 13:18)

B

ACROSS

1. Across a Midianite's shoulders (Isa. 9:4)
3. Precious stone
5. Color
7. We breathe it
9. For ashes or tea
10. "He [Paul] broke it and began to . . ." (Acts 27:35)
11. Job's eyes grew this way (Job 17:7)

DOWN

1. Where David kept his stones
2. Edge
4. Girl's name
5. Bind
6. Almond is one
8. Also
8. Sacrificed instead of Isaac (Gen. 22:13)

C

ACROSS

1. Hoopoe and the . . . (Lev. 11:19)
3. Ahimelech's home (1 Sam. 21:1)
5. Pig's home
7. Fruit
9. . . . out, to supplement
10. An age
11. Full of fish (John 21:6)

DOWN

1 For coal or dust
2. Label
4. Cereal
5. Behold
6. Japanese money
7. Marsh
8. Obtain

D

ACROSS

1. . . . Almighty
3. Tribe of Israel (Num. 1:25)
5. Edge of robe (Exod. 28:34)
7. Final
9. Every
10. Joshua's father (1 Chron. 7:27)
11. Breath of God produces this (Job 37:10)

DOWN

1. With Magog (Rev. 20:8)
2. Father
4. Era
5. Chicken
6. God created him
7. Priest of Shiloh (1 Sam. 1:9)
8. Naphtali is like one set free (Gen. 49:21)

50. CROSSWORD

ACROSS

1. One who does not belong (1 Kings 8:41)
6. Cow's cry
7. Doctor of Laws
10. Owns
12. Paul passed this side of Cyprus and Crete (Acts 27:4,7)
13. Devil
14. Behold
15. Alternative
16. Intelligence
19. Girl's name
21. Another girl's name
22. Bold and free in style
23. "Pick up your . . . and walk" (John 5:8)
25. "He . . . the light from the darkness" (Gen. 1:4)

DOWN

1. Disciples
2. Printer's measure
3. Island in the Hebrides
4. Depart
5. "The whole assembly . . . with a loud voice" (Ezra 10:12)
8. The (French)
9. Greek letter
10. King of Tyre (2 Sam. 5:11)
11. Morning
17. Not out
18. By
20. Negative
23. Mother
24. Baby's thank you

ANSWERS

1. CROSSWORD

ACROSS
1. Multiply
5. Eh
7. Offerings
11. Not
12. Die
13. Pit
14. Duo
16. See

18. Amminadab
20. No
21. Stranger

DOWN
1. Moon
2. Left
3. The
4. Lend

6. Use
8. Forum
9. Reign
10. Gibea
14. Dan
15. Omit
16. Sdog (gods)
17. Eber
19. Ann

2. MISSING WORDS

A 1. Account
2. Believes
3. Commandments
4. Delight
5. Evil
6. Friends
7. Greater
8. Healing
9. Ignore
10. Judged

B 1. Keeping
2. Learn
3. Message
4. Neighbor
5. Obedience
6. Perfect
7. Quench
8. Repentance
9. Strength
10. Treasure

3. BUNCHES OF DATES

A 1. 1788
2. 1865
3. 1961
4. 1226
5. 597
6. 1703

7. 1678
8. 1918

B 1. 1611
2. 1968
3. 1521

4. 1667
5. 1834
6. 1374
7. 12th
8. 1945

4. ALL IN THE AIR

1. Thunder
2. Rain
3. Hurricane
4. Whirlwind
5. Mist
6. Lightning
7. Cloud
8. Snow
9. Breeze
10. Sun

Center column: Hailstones

5. FIVE-LETTER WORDS

A	**B**	**C**	**D**
1. Aaron	1. Exile	1. Third	1. Mercy
2. Never	2. Ephah	2. Derbe	2. Young
3. Rings	3. Honey	3. Endor	3. Gates
4. Samos	4. Yeast	4. Roman	4. Sihon
5. Selah	5. Total	5. Nahum	5. Nisan
6. Hosea	6. Laban	6. Month	6. Naomi
7. Altar	7. Night	7. Heart	7. Idols
8. Rapid	8. Teach	8. Thong	8. Steal
9. Dense	9. Havoc	9. Gihon	9. Latch
10. Elika	10. Chase	10. Nebat	10. Hiram

6. SIX FIVES

ACROSS
1. Jacob
4. Moses
5. Scots

DOWN
1. James
2. Cosmo
3. Buses

7. INSTRUMENTS OF MUSIC

1. Trumpet
2. Lyre
3. Sistrum
4. Harp
5. Flute
6. Tambourine
7. Cymbal
8. Zither
9. Horn
10. Pipe

8. STUDIO FULL OF ART

1. Darting	5. Parting	9. Martyr
2. Hearth	6. Warthog	10. Martha
3. Dearth	7. Quarter	
4. Charter	8. Earthly	

9. A GOOD SCORE

1. 14	4. 7	7. 72	10. 7
2. 20	5. 300	8. 19	11. 10
3. 500	6. 46	9. 5	Total: 1000

10. ALL MADE WELL

1. Blind	5. Crippled	9. Malchus
2. Nain	6. Samaritan	10. Bethesda
3. Dropsy	7. Canaanite	
4. Paralytic	8. Deaf	

Center column: Bartimaeus

11. ONE OF THREE

A		B	
1. Ham		1. Beersheba	
2. Judas		2. Charles Wesley	
3. Peter		3. Charles Spurgeon	
4. Jericho		4. Chloe	
5. Antioch		5. Handel	
6. Patmos		6. Eva Burrows	
7. Bethany		7. Quirinius	
8. Candace		8. Baden-Powell	
9. Gallio		9. Carmel	
10. Elishama		10. Gozan	

C 1. Hamor
   2. Wilson Carlile
   3. Bedford
   4. Epworth
   5. Kayersberg
   6. Malchus
   7. Matthias
   8. Mara
   9. Eglon
   10. Haman

D 1. Adar
   2. William Carey
   3. Ira Sankey
   4. Mary Magdalene
   5. Thomas
   6. Hiram
   7. Plymouth
   8. Latin
   9. Matthew
   10. Zechariah

12. CROSSWORD

ACROSS
1. Egyptians
6. Ait
7. CBE
11. Let
12. Air
13. He
14. Oh
15. Ice
17. Ash
19. Roi
20. (J)ude
22. Disputing

DOWN
1. Exclaimed
2. Pa
3. Time
4. It
5. Searching
8. Be
9. Ether
10. Zahar
16. Urdu
18. So
20. Up
21. Et

13. HIDDEN BIBLE LANDS AND ISLANDS

1. Cyprus
2. Malta
3. Italy
4. Mysia

5. Syria
6. Patmos
7. Moab
8. Egypt

9. Crete
10. Spain

14. WHAT A JUMBLE!

A JUMBLED MOUNTAINS
1. Abarim
2. Olives
3. Carmel
4. Gilboa
5. Moriah
6. Tabor
7. Gerizim

B JUMBLED JEWELS
1. Beryl
2. Jasper
3. Jacinth
4. Emerald
5. Sapphire
6. Amethyst
7. Chrysolite
8. Turquoise

15. BIBLE GROUPS

1. Nazirites
2. Samaritans
3. Sadducees
4. Herodians
5. Looked
6. Scribes
7. Zealots
8. Galileans
9. Pharisees

Center column: Zadokites

16. BIBLE BUILDINGS

1. Booths
2. Wall
3. Barns
4. Fortress
5. Prison
6. Inn
7. Mansions
8. Palace
9. Temple
10. Tents

Center column: Tabernacle

17. A CAGE OF JAYS

1. James
2. Jehu
3. Jidlaph
4. Jonathan
5. Judas
6. Jairus
7. Jethro
8. Jimnah
9. Joseph
10. Jude
11. Jacob
12. Jeremiah
13. Jibsam
14. John
15. Justus

18. HARDLY A CLUE

ACROSS
1. Endurance
6. Ziv
7. Pot
11. Era
12. Ira
13. Be
14. AM
15. Sol

17. Lug
19. Ape
20. Aim
22. Euphrates

DOWN
1. Expensive
2. Uz
3. Riot

4. AV
5. Endangers
8. Or
9. Table
10. Simla
16. Fair
18. Up
20. Ah
21. Ma

19. A HIVE OF BEES

1. Barak
2. Beersheba
3. Bithynia
4. Boaz
5. Buz

6. Barnabas
7. Ben-Hadad
8. Bildad
9. Bozez
10. Bul

11. Baruch
12. Berea
13. Bigthana
14. Boanerges
15. Bubastis

20. SIX IN THIRTY-SIX

A
1. Naaman
2. Joshua
3. Elijah
4. Daniel
5. Joseph
6. Haggai

B
1. Martha
2. Rachel
3. Huldah
4. Esther
5. Miriam
6. Hannah

C
1. Lystra
2. Athens
3. Paphos
4. Tarsus
5. Cyprus
6. Rhodes

D
1. Bethel
2. Gilgal
3. Hebron
4. Mizpah
5. Ziklag
6. Gibeah

E
1. Andrew
2. Philip
3. Thomas
4. Simeon
5. Joseph
6. Jairus

F
1. Isaiah
2. Elisha
3. Gideon
4. Darius
5. Manoah
6. Naboth

21. MOTHERS OF THE BIBLE

1. Rebekah
2. Eunice
3. Hannah
4. Obed
5. Bathsheba
6. Oholibamah
7. Athaliah
8. Mary

Initial letters: Rehoboam

22. BIBLE LANDS

1. Samaria
2. Ethiopia
3. Libya
4. Spain
5. Assyria
6. Persia
7. Arabia
8. Mesopotamia
9. Phoenicia
10. Israel

23. AN ODD ONE OUT

A 1. Psalms (not a New Testament book)
2. Book of Common Prayer (not a Bible version)
3. Aaron (not a son of Jacob)
4. Tiber (not a river in Eden)
5. Kindness (not a gift in 1 Corinthians 13)
6. Coptic (not a language written above the Cross)
7. Joseph (not a son of Noah)
8. Diamond (not on the priestly breastpiece)
9. Snowdon (not a Bible mountain)
10. Dollar (not a Bible coin)

B 1. Portugal (not a Bible country)
2. Mauve (not a Bible color)
3. Gun (not a Bible weapon)
4. Guernsey (not a Bible garment)
5. Rome (not one of the seven churches of Revelation)
6. Maple (not a Bible tree)
7. Piano (not a Bible musical instrument)
8. Sultan (not a Bible royal title)
9. Peter (not an Old Testament character)
10. Buffalo (not a Bible animal)

24. HIDDEN BIBLE FLOWERS AND PLANTS

1. Nard
2. Caraway
3. Cummin
4. Crocus
5. Mandrake
6. Rose
7. Lily
8. Aloes
9. Cassia
10. Dill

25. CROSSWORD

ACROSS
1. Deborah
7. Ave
8. Cry
9. Owe
11. Ami
13. An
14. May
16. No
17. GA
18. Et
19. HP
20. Ton
21. Oa(t)
22. SOS
24. Has
25. MPS
27. Air
28. Palaces

DOWN
1. Dawn
2. Eve
3. Be
4. RC
5. Ara
6. Hymn
9. Oaths
10. AA
12. Iotas
14. Mat
15. Yen
21. Oars
23. Spa
24. Hie
26. SL
27. AC

26. IN ALL DIRECTIONS

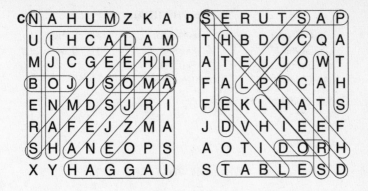

27. SONGS OF PRAISE

1. Soul
2. Night
3. Blessings
4. Life

5. Almighty
6. Blessed
7. Forth tell
8. Redeemer

9. Thousand
10. Gladsome

28. BROKEN NAMES

A Habor
Nile
Pharpar
Kebar
Abana

Pishon
Tigris
Gihon
Jordan
Kishon

B Zephaniah
Malachi
Jonah
Haggai
Joel

Amos
Hosea
Nahum
Zechariah
Habakkuk

29. SIX SEVENS

ACROSS
1. Morning
4. Eliakim
5. Swelter

DOWN
1. Miletus
2. Nahalol
3. Grammar

30. ON THE ROAD

1. Babylon
2. Chariot
3. Jericho
4. Galatia
5. Atharim
6. Horseman
7. Rachel
8. Traveler
9. Rough
10. Crossroads

Center column: Bartimaeus

31. WHO (OR WHAT) ARE WE?

A Redeemer
B Disciple
C Nazareth
D Parables

32. CROSSWORD

ACROSS
1. Jebusites
6. Rot
7. Dry
11. Gnu
12. Air
13. KO
14. Us
15. Edo
17. Tut
19. Spa
20. One
22. Supremacy

DOWN
1. Judgments
2. Ur
3. Soap
4. It
5. Secretary
8. RN
9. Yukon
10. Lasts
16. Cone
18. Up
20. Or
21. EM

33. HIDDEN BIBLE GEMS AND METALS

1. Gold
2. Iron
3. Lead
4. Silver
5. Tin
6. Bronze
7. Copper
8. Topaz
9. Ruby
10. Agate

34. ONE TO NINE

1. Thing
2. Tunics
3. Shelters
4. Headwaters
5. Sparrows
6. Days
7. Times
8. Oxen
9. Cleansed

35. CHANGING LETTERS

A		**B**		**C**		**D**	
SOIL		MEAT		HEAT		MAKE	
FOIL		MOAT		HEAD		SAKE	
FAIL		MOOT		HELD		SALE	
FARL		MOOD		HOLD		SOLE	
FARM		FOOD		COLD		SOLD	

36. ANOTHER GOOD SCORE

1. 1000
2. 3
3. 29
4. 16
5. 40
6. 99
7. 300
8. 8
9. 5
10. 200

Total: 1700

37. SOMETHING OLD

1. Boldness
2. Cold
3. Enfolds
4. Folds
5. Goldsmiths
6. Holding
7. Manifold
8. Oldest
9. Soldier
10. Told
11. Withhold

38. NEIGHBORING KINGS

1. Shalmaneser	5. Pharaoh	9. Sargon
2. Hazael	6. Cyrus	10. Darius
3. Neco	7. Esarhaddon	11. Nebuchad-
4. Benhadad	8. Edrei	nezzar

Center column: Sennacherib

39. PUT ME RIGHT

1. Walk	5. Evil	9. Leaders
2. Leads	6. Take	10. Command
3. Light	7. Selfish	
4. Pure	8. Faithless	

40. CROSSWORD

ACROSS
1. Harvests
7. ie
8. Each
10. Time
12. Thro(ugh)
13. To
14. Rut
15. II(I)
16. Ink
17. Ubi
18. Ti
19. Hot
21. En
22. East
24. Apse
26. Snow
27. Be
28. Statutes

DOWN
1. Hittites
2. Rim
3. Veer
4. Sett (ee)
5. Tah (hat)
6. Scribes
9. Holiness
11. Ionians
19. Htwa (Thaw)
20. Tabu
23. Sot
25. Pet

41. THEY ATE IT ALL

1. Annihilate or assassinate	4. Greatest	8. Consecrated
2. Pomegranate	5. Grateful	9. Indicated
3. Alternated	6. Gateway	10. Created
	7. Plateau	

42. BIBLE TOOLS

1. Nail	5. Shovel	9. Chisel
2. Axe	6. Hoe	10. Plow
3. Hammer	7. Sickle	11. Tongs
4. Sieve	8. Knife	12. Fork

43. OLD ENGLISH HYMNS

A			**B**	
1.	Father		1.	World
2.	Ages		2.	King
3.	Great		3.	Bright
4.	Promised		4.	Royal
5.	Shepherd		5.	Perishing
6.	Heavenly		6.	Spend
7.	Time		7.	Gladsome
8.	Anchor		8.	Crib
9.	Grave		9.	Midnight
10.	Battle			
11.	Wondrous			
12.	Over			

44. SPELL A NAME

A Peter	**D** Caleb
B Hosea	**E** Felix
C Spain	

45. PUT ME RIGHT AGAIN

1. Blessed	5. Forsaken	9. Pants
2. Persecute	6. Learning	10. Oppressed
3. Lower	7. Ignorant	
4. Helpless	8. Charge	

46. CROSSWORD

ACROSS
1. Perverse
6. Ai
7. It
9. Unfailing
13. Gut
14. Rag
15. Sky
16. His
18. Emp(ty)
20. Macedonia

23. (H)oe
24. Wo
25. Strength

DOWN
1. Plug
2. Raft
3. Via
4. Ril(l)
5. Stir
8. Egg

10. Nubia
11. Inked
12. Naomi
16. HMS
17. Scot
18. Enog
19. Path
21. Eer
22. Own

47. MORE MISSING WORDS

A 1. Atoning
2. Blesses
3. Careful
4. Desire
5. Exalted
6. Faith
7. Gracious
8. Honor
9. Idle
10. Joyful
11. Kindness
12. Loving

B 1. Marvelous
2. Needs
3. Obey
4. Purify
5. Quarrel
6. Righteousness
7. Salvation
8. Trust
9. Unfailing
10. Victory
11. Weak
12. Zeal

48. JUMBLED KINGS OF ISRAEL AND JUDAH

1. Jeroboam
2. Jehoram
3. Solomon
4. Hoshea

5. Jehoiachin
6. Zachariah
7. Pekahiah
8. Rehoboam

9. Jehoshaphat
10. Manasseh

49. THREE-LETTER CROSSWORDS

A ACROSS	B ACROSS	C ACROSS	D ACROSS
1. Hay	1. Bar	1. Bat	1. God
3. Tea	3. Gem	3. Nob	3. Gad
5. Hin	5. Tan	5. Sty	5. Hem
7. Sos	7. Air	7. Fig	7. End
9. Oak	9. Urn	9. Eke	9. All
10. Tar	10. Eat	10. Eon	10. Nun
11. Yew	11. Dim	11. Net	11. Ice

DOWN	DOWN	DOWN	DOWN
1. Hot	1. Bag	1. Bin	1. Gog
2. Yea	2. Rim	2. Tab	2. Dad
4. Ehi	4. Eva	4. Oat	4. Age
5. Hat	5. Tie	5. See	5. Hen
6. Nor	6. Nut	6. Yen	6. Man
7. Sky	7. And	7. Fen	7. Eli
8. Sew	8. Ram	8. Get	8. Doe

50. CROSSWORD

ACROSS	DOWN
1. Foreigner	1. Followers
6. Moo	2. Em
7. LLD	3. Iona
10. Has	4. Go
12. Lee	5. Responded
13. Imp	8. Le
14. Lo	9. Delta
15. Or	10. Hiram
16. Wit	11. Am
19. Ann	17. In
21. Ena	18. Near
22. Mod	20. No
23. Mat	23. Ma
25. Separated	24. Ta

1. CROSSWORD

Across

1. A false witness tells them (Prov. 12:17)
4. Where Paul was imprisoned (Acts 28:16)
7. "They have . . . the Lord out of the tomb" (John 20:2)
8. Canaanite god
10. Not rich
12. Before Bethel (Gen. 35:7)
13. Short view
14. Salvation Army
15. Eggs
16. Father of Joshua
17. Us
18. Little child
19. King of Bashan
21. Naggai's father (Luke 3:25)
23. Shortened Egyptian town
25. Carried
26. Elders were appointed in every one (Titus 1:5)
27. No one can do this to the tongue (James 3:8)

Down

1. Part of the ear
2. Greek letter
3. It comes from the Lord (Jonah 2:9)
4. God will not reject this heart
5. Shemed built this city (1 Chron. 8:12)
6. Priest
9. Grown with myrrh (Song of Songs 4:14)
11. White and flaky, vocative
17. Where a cloud was rising (Luke 12:54)
20. Through the narrow one (Matt. 7:13)
22. Cricket term
24. Mass of water

2. AN ALPHABET OF HUSBANDS AND WIVES

In the space provided write the name or word.

1. Husband of Sapphira (Acts 5:1)   **A** ....
2. King Agrippa's queen
   (Acts 25:13)   **B** ....
3. Ephrath's second husband
   (1 Chron. 2:19)   **C** ....
4. Michal married him
   (1 Sam. 18:27)   **D** ....
5. Adam's wife   **E** ....
6. Druscilla married this governor
   (Acts 24:24)   **F** ....
7. Hosea's wayward wife
   (Hos. 1:3)   **G** ....
8. Wife of Elkanah (1 Sam. 1:2)   **H** ....
9. Rebecca's husband
   (Gen. 25:20)   **I** ....
10. Chuza married her (Luke 8:3)   **J** ....
11. A man's wife is his next of   **K** ....
12. Prophet Deborah's husband
    (Judg. 4:4)   **L** ....
13. Married to Nahor (Gen. 11:29)   **M** ....
14. Abigail's first husband
    (2 Sam. 2:2)   **N** ....
15. Acsah married him
    (Josh. 15:17)   **O** ....
16. Aquila's wife (Acts 18:12)   **P** ....
17. A king's wife is usually   **Q** ....
18. Wife of Boaz (Ruth 4:13)   **R** ....
19. Married to Abram (Gen. 11:29)   **S** ....
20. Benabinadab married Solomon's
    daughter (1 Kings 4:11)   **T** ....

21. Bathsheba's first husband
     (2 Sam. 11:3)   **U** ....
22. Queen to the king of Persia
     (Esther 1:9)   **V** ....
23. A man's wife is always a   **W** ....
24. Vashti's royal husband
     (Esther 1:1)   **X** ....
25. These women should be care-
     ful to love their husbands
     (Titus 2:4)   **Y** ....
26. Husband to Elizabeth
     (Luke 1:5)   **Z** ....

3. Workers with Paul

ADD letters to replace the stars and discover the name of Paul's helpers mentioned in 2 Timothy and Philemon.

1.	E	*	*	U	L	U	*				
2.	*	R	*	H	I	*	P	*	S		
3.	T	*	*	H	I	*	U	*			
4.	O	*	*	S	*	M	*	*			
5.	*	R	*	S	*	*	L	*	A		
6.	*	L	*	U	D	*	*				
7.	A	*	*	S	*	A	R	*	*	U	*
8.	*	R	A	*	*	U	*				
9.	T	*	O	*	H	*	M	*	S		
10.	*	N	*	*	I	*	H	O	*	U	*

4. PSALM FIFTEEN

ONE word is filled in to help. All other words can be found in Psalm 15.

5. EIGHT DAYS OF WONDER

WRITE one letter of the answer to the numbered clues in each square. When all squares are filled, the letters in the box will answer the unnumbered clue.

1. He saw the sun stand still. (Josh. 10:12)
2. What the Jews of Nehemiah's day made the Sabbath day. (Neh. 13:17)
3. "In that day" who will hear the words of the scroll? (Isa. 29:18)
4. What sort of day will the day of the Lord be? (Joel 2:31)
5. Who instituted the Day of Atonement? (Lev. 16:34)
6. How many days did Jesus teach in the temple? (Luke 19:47)
7. Kings will be drawn to the dawning of this day. (Isa. 60 GOOD NEWS)
8. Until which day was the tomb of Jesus guarded? (Matt. 27:64)

Initial column: We will have confidence on this day. (1 John 4:17)

6. REGROUP THE LETTERS

REGROUP the letters in the following sentences to form well-known Bible verses.

1. Eve ryo new hoc all sont hena meo fth elor dwil lbes aved.
2. Fort hew age so fsi nisd eat hbutt heg if tof go diset ern all ife.
3. Ha vemer cyon meo go dac cord in gto yo urun fa ilin glove.
4. Ta stean dse etha tth elo rdi sgo od.
5. Theh arve sti splen tifu lbu tthew ork ersa ref ew.
6. Chr istje susca mein tot hew or ldt osa ves inn ers.
7. Ic and oev eryt hin gthro ugh hi mwhog ive smest ren gth.

7. ALONG THE ROAD

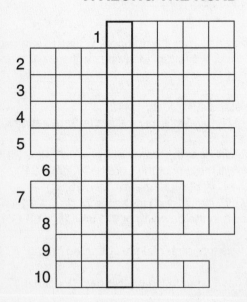

1. What sort of road leads to destruction? (Matt. 7:13)
2. When the Gaza road is not used. (Acts 8 GOOD NEWS)

3. Rachel was buried by the side of the road to this place. (Gen. 35:19)
   4. On what sort of road (route) did the eastern star-studiers return from Bethlehem? (Matt. 2:12)
   5. The highway where no wicked fool travels. (Isa. 35:8)
   6. On what sort of road was a priest going down? (Luke 10:31)
   7. The people spread these on the road on Palm Sunday. (Luke 19:35)
   8. On what road did marauders commit murder? (Hos. 6:9)
   9. Hagar was found by a spring on this road. (Gen. 16:7)
   10. The Israelites took this road and met King Og. (Num. 21:33)

Center column: The beggar who sat by the Jericho road. (Mark 10:46)

8. PUT ME RIGHT

CORRECT the wrong word in each verse.

1. I will be careful to live a blameless life. (Ps. 101:2)
2. A man carrying a bar of water will meet you. (Mark 14:13)
3. At once they left their nests and followed him. (Matt. 4:20)
4. He saw the disciples straining at the oaks, because the wind was against them. (Mark 6:48)
5. He guides me in patches of righteousness for his name's sake. (Ps. 23:3)
6. You prefer a table before me in the presence of my enemies. (Ps. 23:5)
7. The Lord has compassion on those who fear men. (Ps. 103:13)

9. CROSSWORD

Across

1. The gates were shut (Josh. 6:1)
7. Preposition
8. Cereal without end
10. Morning
11. Spoil
12. Mother
13. Exist
14. Strong wind (Acts 27:14)
16. Gone by
17. Snake
18. Proceed
20. King of Egypt (2 Kings 17:4)
21. Not them
22. By way of
23. On Swiss cars
24. "Come to . . . all you who are weary" (Matt. 11:28)
25. Georgia
27. A wicked one (Luke 19:22)

Down

2. French for "and"
3. Italian capital
4. Plenty in Egypt
5. Shout for joy
6. Raised from the dead (John 11:43)
9. Old Testament book
13. Marsh
15. Headless mountain
19. . . . and above
20. Heroic story
24. Myself
26. Indefinite article

10. WHO ARE WE?

A   My first is in **NAAMAN** and clearly in **MAID**,
My next is in **PROFIT** but never in **TRADE**;
My third's used in **JEHU**, **JERUSALEM** too,
My fourth comes in **DONKEY** and centers in **GNU**;
My fifth is in **WATER** but never in **WINE**,
My sixth's in **ABEL** as well as in **CAIN**;
My next's not in **CLOUDY** but stands out in **FINE**,
My last's not in **WIDOW** but doubles in **NAIN**.
        My whole's a large hill.

B   My first comes in **EGYPT** but never in **NILE**,
My second's in **HAMMER** but never in **FILE**;
My next shines in **DARKNESS** as well as in **DAY**,
My fourth's in the **POTTER** but not in the **CLAY**;
In **SILVER** my fifth comes and clearly in **TIN**,
My next is in **GOODNESS** as well as in **SIN**;
At **EVEN** my seventh shines but never at **MORN**,
My last is in **BARLEY** but missing in **CORN**.
        My whole's a religious group in
        New Testament times.

C   My first is in **DUTY** but not in a **GAME**,
My next is in **TITLE** but not in a **NAME**;
My third is in **SIX** and is clearly in **SEVEN**,
The next is in **CHRISTIAN** but never in **HEAVEN**;
My fifth's used in **DAVID** but missed out in **SAUL**,
My next is in **PETER** as well as in **PAUL**;
My seventh's in **ELI**, in **SAMUEL**, and **LUKE**,
My last is in **COMPLIMENT** and in **REBUKE**.
        My whole is just one of the
        followers of Christ.

D   My first is in **JORDAN** as well as **ISRAEL**,
        RAIN never has my second but comes clear in **GALE**;
        My third's not in **NOSES** but stands out in **HEAD**,
        My next comes in **YELLOW** but never in **RED**;
        In **GIVEN** no fifth comes though clearly in **BOUGHT**,
        My sixth is in **HARBOR** as well as in **PORT**;
        In **ANCHOR** my next lies as well as in **BOAT**,
        My last's not in **CASTLE** but lies in the **MOAT**.
            My whole was Solomon's son.

11. TRIPLE COLUMN

THE center three columns are the same and spell the name of a well-known woman.

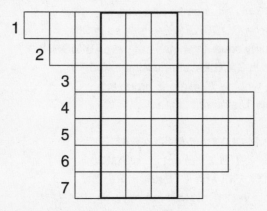

1. Where Jonah was told to go (Jon. 1:2)
2. "I will . . . pests from devouring your crops" (Mal. 3:11)
3. God was pleased to do this with his Son in Paul (Gal. 1:16)
4. Never take this (Rom. 12:19)
5. For Tyre it was the harvest of the Nile (Isa. 23:3)
6. Famine was of this quality everywhere (Gen. 41:56)
7. Churches in the province of Asia (Rev. 1:4)

12. HOW MANY?

WRITE the figure in the space provided at the end of the question. If you add up the column from 2 to 12 you will find the total to be the answer to the first question.

1. How many years are like a day? (2 Peter 3:8) ....
2. How old was Seth when Enosh was born? (Gen. 5:6) ....
3. For how many shekels of silver did Abraham buy some property in Machpelah? (Gen. 23:16) ....
4. How many sons had Zebedee? (Luke 5:10) ....
5. For how many hours were the Ephesians shouting for Artemis? (Acts 19:34) ....
6. For how many years did Asa rule in Jerusalem? (1 Kings 15:10) ....
7. How many years had Aeneas been bedridden before he met Peter? (Acts 9:33) ....
8. For how many years did the Israelites eat manna? (Exod. 16:35) ....
9. How many apostles did Jesus choose? (Mark 3:14) ....
10. How many horsemen accompanied Paul to Caesarea? (Acts 23:23) ....
11. How many years did Solomon take to build the temple and his palace? (1 Kings 9:10) ....
12. How many of Gideon's men lapped water in their hands? (Judg. 7:6) ....

13. AGES PAST AND PRESENT

EVERY answer contains the letters **AGE**, and the initial letters spell yet another word containing these letters.

1. The age found in the temple that had to be repaired. (2 Kings 12:5)
2. Christ is this age of the invisible God. (Col. 1:15)
3. God promised to remove this age of beasts from the land. (Lev. 26:6)
4. This age escorted by sixty warriors belonged to Solomon. (Song of Songs 3:7)
5. Someone who is too old.
6. This age takes a medical covering off.
7. We must rid ourselves of such things as this age. (Col. 3:8)
8. We must not take this age of each other. (Lev. 25:14)
9. This age is given as security.
10. The Bereans received the message with this age. (Acts 17:11)
11. This age once held a title.

Initial letters: Any who are afraid must not be this age. (Deut. 1:21)

14. ON THE FARM

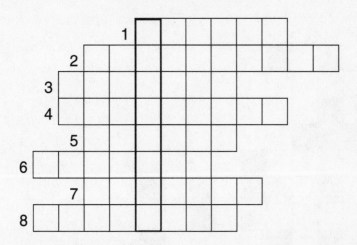

1. Boaz gave Ruth six measures of this. (Ruth 3:15)
2. Swords will be beat into. . . . (Isa. 2:4)
3. God will repay for the years they have eaten. (Joel 2:25)
4. A fork for threshing the grain (Matt. 3:12)
5. Food for oxen and donkeys (Isa. 30:24)
6. The smallest seed (Matt. 13:31)
7. They reaped a fruitful one. (Ps. 107:37)
8. Noah was the first to plant one. (Gen. 9:20)

Center column: This stone must not be moved. (Deut. 27:17)

15. MINI-CROSSWORDS

Across

1. More than better
3. . . . of meeting (Lev. 1:1)
5. Depart
6. Place of honey (Prov. 24:13)
8. King of Judah in Isaiah's time (Isa. 7:1)
10. Footwear (Isa. 5:27)
12. Morning
13. School period

Down

1. Wash place (John 13:10)
2. Sing a new one (Ps. 96:1)
4. Two Marys left it in a hurry (Matt. 28:8)
6. Do this with lots (Prov. 16:33)
7. The reformed tombdweller was in his right one (Mark 5:15)
8. Wheel center (1 Kings 7:30)
9. Cain's father (Gen. 4:1)
11. Headless head covering

B

Across

1. Brother of James (Jude 1)
3. It had human eyes (Dan. 7:8)
5. Not yes
6. Say nothing here (2 Sam. 1:20)
8. Crops are ready (John 4:35)
10. Persian emperor (Dan. 5:31)
12. King of Bashan (Num. 21:33)
13. Sound of thunder (Rev. 14:2)

Down

1. Gospel writer
2. Mend
4. Flood survivor (Gen. 8:13)
6. Father of Menahem (2 Kings 15:17)
7. Had a king named Hiram (2 Chron. 2:3)
8. On Sunday Jesus . . . (Mark 16:9)
9. One at Siloam (John 9:7)
11. . . . and down

C

Across

1. Tied up in the village (Mark 11:2)
3. Father of Ahinadab (1 Kings 4:14)
5. One time
6. Repent, then, and . . . to God (Acts 3:19)
8. Third man (Gen. 4:2)
10. City of Ammon (Deut. 3:11)
12. To be
13. Nabel was surly and . . . (1 Sam. 25:3)

Down

1. Baby bed
2. Magnetic stone
4. Bought five yoke of . . . (Luke 14:19)
6. Ottoman
7. Father ordered the best one (Luke 15:22)
8. Pain
9. Girl's name
11. . . . I not free? (1 Cor. 9:1)

16. CHANGING LETTERS

CHANGE one letter at a time to find a connected word

A T A M E

- - - - - - - - - -   Now is the . . . of God's favor. (2 Cor. 6:2)
- - - - - - - - - -   Roof covering (Luke 5:19)
- - - - - - - - - -   Trick
- - - - - - - - - -   These animals pant for you. (Joel 1:20)

B W O R K

- - - - - - - - - -   Plant
- - - - - - - - - -   Ancient part of "to be"
- - - - - - - - - -   Men from here were appalled at Job's fate. (Job 18:20)
- - - - - - - - - -   Seventh day (Exod. 31:15)

C S E E K

- - - - - - - - - -   Sowed in the field (Matt. 13:31)
- - - - - - - - - -   . . . my messenger ahead (Matt. 11:10)
- - - - - - - - - -   Ward off
- - - - - - - - - -   Discover

D C O M E

- - - - - - - - - -   Heart of an apple
- - - - - - - - - -   Take . . . of my sheep. (John 21:16)
- - - - - - - - - -   Carried the ark of God (1 Chron. 13:7)
- - - - - - - - - -   Separate

17. AN ALPHABET OF BIBLE MEN

WRITE the name or word in the space provided.

1. **A** is for .... the first man with sheep (Gen. 4:2)
2. **B** is for .... with a donkey to keep (Num. 22:21)
3. **C** is for .... a spy good and true (Num. 14:38)
4. **D** is for .... sends greetings to you (Col. 4:14)
5. **E** is for .... a fighter left-handed (Judg. 3:15)
6. **F** is for .... a hearing demanded (Acts 25:12)
7. **G** is for .... the teacher of Paul (Acts 22:3)
8. **H** is for .... a priest in God's call (2 Kings 22:4)
9. **I** is for .... the father of Esau (Gen. 25:21, 25)
10. **J** is for .... the father of twelve more (Gen. 35:22)
11. **K** is for .... rebelled, was destroyed (Jude 11)
12. **L** is for .... with Jacob annoyed (Gen. 31:31)
13. **M** is for .... long-living man (Gen. 5:27)
14. **N** is for .... head of a clan (Num. 26:40)
15. **O** is for .... King Ahab's old dad (1 Kings 16:28)
16. **P** is for .... whose judgment was bad (Luke 23:24)
17. **Q** is for .... sends wishes to Rome (Rom. 16:24)
18. **R** is for .... from Simon's own home (Mark 15:21)
19. **S** is for .... first martyr for Christ (Acts 7:59)
20. **T** is for .... by doubting enticed (John 20:27)
21. **U** is for .... a king at sixteen (2 Chron. 26:1)
22. **V** is for .... to Canaan unseen (Num. 13:14)
23. **W** is for .... Jacob's gift to Sychar (John 4:6)
24. **X** is for .... from Persia afar (Esther 1:1)
25. **Y** is for .... Jeremiah wore this around his neck to warn the Israelites (Jer. 27:2)
26. **Z** is for .... shared Saul's property (2 Sam. 19:17)

18. HIDDEN BIBLE GEMS

FIND the jewels hidden in the sentences below.

1. The way to life is through a gate that is narrow.
2. To reach the top a zealous aim is needed.
3. In Ezekiel's day you might rub your skin with olive oil.
4. With a sharp ear listen to God's word.
5. Animals may cry stalking through the land.
6. The father of Jacob was Isaac or Alexander.
7. Do not blame thy stewards.
8. Rajas persisted in India; emperors in Rome.
9. His psalms have given David (Di) a mondial influence.

19. PSALM TWENTY-FOUR

TWO words are filled in to help. All other words can be found in Psalm 24:1–6

20. WHAT A JUMBLE!

UNJUMBLE the following lines to find Old Testament places.

1. A MEOMIA POST
2. A BLONI BAY
3. VINE HEN
4. A MESSER
5. OHE OILS PIL
6. EZEE BORING
7. HE BARS BEE
8. THE HEM BEL
9. HART MAZE
10. RAZE PATH H
11. RULE JAMES
12. AS A RIMA

21. JUMBLED CHURCHES

UNJUMBLE the following lines and you will have the names of the seven churches of the Revelation.

1. HE SUES P
2. Y ARMS N
3. GUME PRAM
4. I TRY A HAT
5. S S RAID
6. ICED ALOA
7. DIAL A HIP HELP

22. BROTHERS AND SISTERS

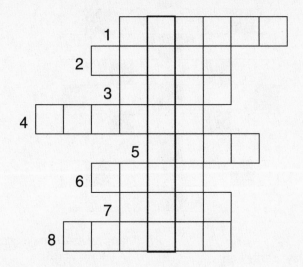

1. One of Benjamin's brothers (Gen. 29:33)
2. Aaron's brother (Exod. 4:14)
3. Brother of Jacob (Gen. 25:26)
4. Sister to Moses (Exod. 15:20)
5. Abel's brother (Gen. 4:1)
6. Brother of James (Matt. 4:21)
7. Martha's sister (John 11:1)
8. Peter's brother (Matt. 4:18).

Center column: One of Naphtali's brothers (Gen. 30:18)

23. CROSSWORD

1		2	3		4	5		6
		7						
8	9				10		11	
12			13				14	
	15				16			
17			18				19	20
21		22			23	24		
		25						
26					27			

Across

1. Partly clay, partly iron (Dan. 2:41)
4. Boat builder (Gen. 7:1)
7. Dead language
8. Encampment with springs and palm trees (Exod.15:27)
10. Jeremiah in one underground (Jer. 37:16)
12. Act
13. Fuss
14. Not down
15. Moses rested in a basket covered with this (Exod. 2:3)
16. Unclear
17. South Africa
18. Anger
19. Greek letter
21. Make with wool
23. Pulpy food
25. Father of Amos (Luke 3:25)
26. Dove's noise (Isa. 38:14)
27. "Many advisers make victory . . ." (Prov. 11:14)

Down

1. "A donkey . . . there" (Matt. 21:2)
2. Father of Hophni (1 Sam. 1:3)
3. Jesus told of a good one (Luke 10:33)
4. Came to Jesus at night (John 3:2)
5. Number of true gods (1 Cor. 8:6)
6. Aid
9. An Horite chief (Gen. 36:29)
11. These of clay become pottery
17. Remove cream from milk
20. Island
22. Girl's name
24. Australian bird

24. ONE OF THREE

A 1. Which is the name of a clan of temple workmen? (Neh. 7:51) Gaza, Gazzam, or Gazelle
2. Name a city belonging to the tribe of Benjamin. (Josh. 18:24) Ophel, Ophni, or Ophir
3. Who was a prophet in the time of David? (2 Sam. 12:1) Nathan, Nahum, or Nahor
4. Name a man who persevered in times of trial. (James 5:11) Nob, Job, or Mob
5. Name a Canaanite god. (1 Kings 16:31) Baal, Bela, or Bul
6. Who was the wife of Cuza? (Luke 8:3) Joash, Joahaz, or Joanna
7. Name a son of Joseph. (Num. 13:7) Og, Agag, or Igal
8. Which was a mountain? (Num. 20:22) Zoar, Hor, or Dor
9. Who was a high priest? (Neh. 3:1) Elijah, Eliashib, or Elisha
10. Name a town near Ibleam. (2 Kings 9:27) Ur, Gur, or Hur

B 1. Name the first-born of Milcah. (Gen. 22:21) Uz, Buz, or Luz
2. Who was Lamech's wife? (Gen. 4:19) Priscilla, Zillah, or Aquila
3. Name the first murderer. (Gen. 4:8) Ain, Nain, or Cain
4. Name a river in Gozan. (2 Kings 17:6) Habor, Tabor, or Nahor
5. Name the kingdom ruled by Melchizedek. (Gen. 14:18) Elim, Helam, or Salem
6. Who was a Hivite? (Gen. 36:2) Zibeon, Gideon, or Midian
7. Who was the world's first great conqueror? (Gen. 10:9) Arod, Nimrod, or Herod
8. Name the island where John was imprisoned. (Rev. 1:9) Patmos, Amos, or Paphos
9. Who was the brother of Alexander? (Mark 15:21) Rufus, Lucius, or Publius
10. Name a prisoner with Paul. (Rom. 16:7) Troas, Phinehas, or Junias

C 1. What was the name of the father of Enosh? (Gen. 4:26) Heth, Beth, or Seth
2. What was the name of an Ammonite city? (2 Sam. 11:1) Raamah, Rabbah, or Rapah

3. What was the name of Jacob's wife? (Gen. 29:23)
   Lehi, Levi, or Leah

4. What was the name of a son of Shem? (Gen. 10:22)
   Lud, Lod, or Luz

5. Who was a king of Israel? (2 Kings 8:16) Joram, Jotham, or Hotham

6. Who was a priest in Jerusalem? (2 Kings 11:4)
   Jehoichin, Jehoiakim, or Jehoiada

7. What was the name of an official in Hezekiah's court?
   (2 Kings 18:18) Sheba, Shebna, or Shebat

8. Who was the son of Shallum? (2 Chron. 28:12) Jehizkiah, Jeremiah, or Jekamiah

9. Who was the last king of Judah? (1 Kings 22:11)
   Hilkiah, Hezekiah, or Zedekiah

10. Who was Elisha's father? (1 Kings 19:16) Shaphat, Shaphan, or Shashak

D 1. Who was one of David's priests? (2 Sam. 20:26)
   Ira, Iri, or Iru?

2. Who revolted against David? (2 Sam. 20:1) Tebah, Ziba, or Sheba

3. Who played a low-pitched harp? (1 Chron. 15:21)
   Amaziah, Ahaziah, or Azaziah

4. Name David's eldest son. (2 Sam. 3:2) Amon, Ammon, or Amnon

5. What was the name of a brook? (1 Sam. 30:9)
   Besor, Beer, or Beor

6. Name a place with twelve springs of water. (Exod. 15:27)
   Elim, Elah, or Elam

7. Name Samuel's mother. (1 Sam. 1:20) Hanani, Hananiah, or Hannah

8. Who played a high-pitched harp? (1 Chron. 15:18)
   Jael, Joel, or Jehiel

9. Who helped to rebuild Jerusalem? (Neh. 3:7) Judah, Jadon, or Judas

10. Name a son of Ishmael (1 Chron 1:30) Dura, Dumah, or Bumah

25. THE LORD'S PRAYER

TWO words are filled in to help. All words can be found in the Lord's Prayer in Matthew 6:9–13.

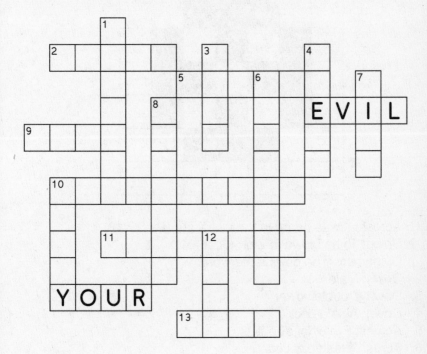

26. CROSSWORD

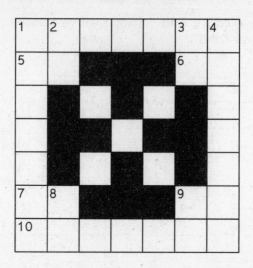

1. Across: It was heard in the whirlwind (Ps. 77:18)
   Down: To be blown in Zion (Joel 2:1)
   Diagonally: The devil is the worst
2. Down: Male
3. Down: Double vowel
4. Down: Also a cock
5. Across: Prefix for about
6. Across: Headless lion
7. Across: Follow dinn and supp
8. Down: Double consonant
9. Across: as 3 down
   Down: as 6 across
10. Diagonally: One who tries to catch animals
    Across: Judas the most well known (Luke 6:16)

27. REGROUP MORE LETTERS

REGROUP the following letters to form well-known Bible verses.

1. Bles seda ret hepe ace ma kers fo rth eyw ill beca lleds on sofg od.
2. Gre ate rlo veha snoo net hant hi stha the la ydow nhi sli fef or hisf ri ends.
3. Su rely go odnes sand lo vew ill fo llo wmea llth eda ysof myl ife.
4. Yo urwo rdi sal amp tomy fe eta ndal ight form ypa th.
5. Con sec ratey ours elve sfo rtom or rowt helo rdwil ldoa mazin gthin gsam on gyou.
6. No wist heti meo fgo dsfa vou rno wist heda yofs alv at ion.
7. Beo nyo urgu ards tan dfir mint hefa ith be me nof cou rageb est rong.

28. STRIP WORDS

A main word fills each strip and can be built up by answering the two or three clues for each puzzle, placing the letters in the numbered squares.

A

1	2	3	4	5	6	7

Main word (1–7): unending
7, 3, 2: allow; 1, 6, 4, 5: obtain for work

B

1	2	3	4	5	6	7	8

Main word (1–8): disciple
6, 7: not they; 2, 1: origin; 8, 5, 3, 4: list of names

C

1	2	3	4	5	6	7	8	9

Main word (1–9): love
2, 8, 4: enemy; 3, 1, 5, 6: reality; 7, 9: not out

D

1	2	3	4	5	6	7	8	9	10

Main word (1–10): loyalty to country
1, 5, 10: length of life; 3, 7, 9, 4: open fabric; 8, 6, 2: nothing

E

1	2	3	4	5	6	7	8	9	10	11

Main word (1–11): recognize
7, 5, 2, 3: fasten; 4, 8, 6: fresh; 1, 10, 11, 9: old

29. ODD ONE OUT

ONE word in each list does not fit into the pattern.

A 1. Blacksmith, carpenter, electrician
2. Weymouth, Moffatt, Thomas
3. Matthew, Mark, Romans
4. Athens, Bethlehem, Nazareth
5. Adam, Paul, Mary
6. Galilee, Jordan, Nile
7. Peter, James, Timothy
8. Exodus, Psalms, Jude
9. Moses, David, Cornelius
10. Wise, surprise, televise

B 1. Saul, Isaiah, Jeremiah
2. Jeroboam, Solomon, Ezekiel
3. Lois, Eunice, Martha
4. Philistines, Gad, Zebulun
5. Germany, Assyria, Judah
6. Greek, Hebrew, French
7. Lost coin, lost sheep, lost feather
8. Wisdom, faith, hope
9. God, silver, myrrh
10. Easter, Christmas, New Year

30. SIX-LETTER WORDS

FILL in the squares according to the clues by the side of each line. The last letter of the first line is the same as the first letter of the second line, and so on.

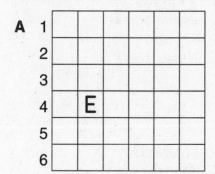

A

1. Acts 9:36
2. Hebrews 11:32
3. One of Nahum 3:15
4. Mark 11:11
5. Second book
6. 2 Peter 1:18

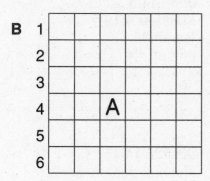

B

1. Amos 3:14
2. Judges 17:9
3. James 5:17
4. Luke 11:13
5. 2 Kings 5:1
6. Luke 3:25

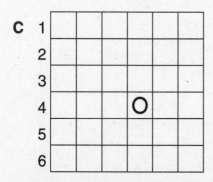

C

1. Revelation 3:1
2. Revelation 2:8
3. Acts 17:16
4. Mark 15:40
5. 2 Timothy 1:5
6. Acts 21:18

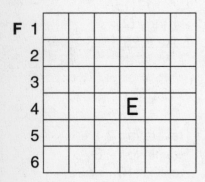

D

1					
2					
3		O			
4					
5					
6					

1. Acts 16:21
2. Luke 2:25
3. 2 Kings 9:21
4. Psalm 10:14
5. Acts 3:19
6. Never lose it

E

1					
2					
3		T			
4					
5					
6					

1. Luke 8:32
2. John 9:7
3. John 11:5
4. Matthew 4:18
5. Isaiah 28:5
6. James 4:4

F

1					
2					
3					
4		E			
5					
6					

1. Joshua 14:15
2. Not one person
3. Over there
4. Annul
5. 2 Timothy 3:11
6. 1 Kings 11:30

31. LOST WORDS

A well known Bible verse will appear as you fill in the missing words and read them downwards. Also add the verse numbers.

1. In all things . . . works for the good of those who love him. (Rom. 8)
2. God . . . light; in him there is no darkness. (1 John 1)
3. He is . . . God and we are the people of his pasture. (Ps. 95)
4. He is my . . . and my fortress, my God, in whom I trust. (Ps. 91)
5. I am the true vine . . . my Father is the gardener. (John 15)
6. He gives . . . to the weary and increases the power of the weak. (Isa. 40)
7. Each of us will give . . . account of himself to God. (Rom. 14)
8. Jesus Christ is the same yesterday and today and for. . . . (Heb. 3)
9. [Christ] who gave himself for our sins to rescue us from the . . . evil age. (Gal. 1)
10. You are my . . . and my deliverer. (Ps. 40)
11. Love does not delight . . . evil but rejoices with the truth. (1 Cor. 13)
12. You are my fortress, my refuge in times of. . . . (Ps. 59)

32. A COLLECTION OF ACTS

EVERY answer contains the letters ACT, and the initial letters spell yet another word.

1. Jews wear them on their foreheads. (Matt. 23:5)
2. An atomic pile
3. This act describes the teaching about God. (Titus 2:10)
4. A plant with many spines
5. Moses needed this in leading the Israelites.
6. Untouched, complete
7. This act concerns a servant. (Isa. 21:11)
8. To be correct

Initial letters: Put into this act what you learn. (Phil. 4:9)

33. BY THE WATER

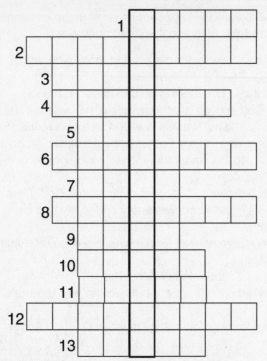

1. Shipwrecked Paul landed here. (Acts 28:1)
2. Jesus called four by Sea of Galilee. (Matt. 4:18)
3. David's descendants will be as many as the grains of this. (Jer. 33:22)
4. Also called Tiberias (John 6:1)
5. Let down for a catch (Luke 5:4)
6. Paul visited here before Cyprus. (Acts 13:4)
7. Made of oak trees (Ezek. 27:6)
8. Used by Jesus to make a fire (John 21:9 GOOD NEWS)
9. The waves broke over it. (Mark 4:37)
10. Large fish swallowed him. (Jonah 1:17)
11. Mediterranean island (Acts 27:7)
12. Sea monster (Ps. 104:26)
13. They obeyed Jesus. (Matt. 8:27)

Center column: Water from Palestine to Spain

34. IN ALL DIRECTIONS

THE words appear forward, backward, upward, downward, or diagonally. Circle each word.

A

Eight Kings of Judah

```
M A H T O J O H
A M A C D A L E
O E B H F M I Z
B Q I B A A M E
O K J K X Z P K
H S A O J I D I
E N M L W A S A
R S T P Q H C H
```

HEZEKIAH   AHAZ   ABIJAM
REHOBOAM   AMON   JOTHAM
AMAZIAH   ASA

B

Eight Kings of Israel

```
B I G H U H E J
J R O A D W E H
E M Z Q P R C A
H I N M O K O I
O Z M B R S L Z
R N O W B A H A
A A B J O A S H
M A F G B P T A
```

JEHORAM   JEHU   ZIMRI
AHAZIAH   AHAB   JOASH
JEROBOAM   OMNI

C

Eleven of Jacob's Sons

```
I L A T H P A N
Q S I M E O N U
J O S E P H M L
U P N A D O E U
D W C Z C V L B
A K X S I H G E
H R E H S A A Z
N E B U E R D R
```

NAPHTALI   DAN   SIMEON   ASHER
ZEBULUN   LEVI   REUBEN   JUDAH
ISSACHAR   GAD   JOSEPH

D

Ten New Testament Books

```
P Z W K N L P E
M H T O R H A D
A M I I E E O U
T A T L T M T J
T R U A E U A O
H K S C P M S B
E B A T E K O E
W C E S D R T N
```

JOHN   JUDE   PETER   ACTS
JAMES   MARK   TITUS   LUKE
MATTHEW   PHILEMON

E

Ten Old Testament Books

```
N A H U M W X P
G E N E S I S Z
H I H E O A I H
A R Z E L P S A
G U A M M S A C
G C S T V I I I
A I H C A L A M
I D F R U T H H
```

RUTH	NAHUM	GENESIS
EZRA	HAGGAI	MALACHI
MICAH	PSALMS	NEHEMIAH
ISAIAH		

F

Eleven Towns of Paul's Travels

```
I H A R T S Y L
Q C O R I N T H
R O O D E R B E
H I S N E H T A
O T W C I R F E
D N F L O U Z R
E A M A K S M E
S U S E H P E B
```

ANTIOCH	LYSTRA	DERBE
CORINTH	ATHENS	COS
EPHESUS	BEREA	TROAS
ICONIUM	RHODES	

G

Eleven More Places in Paul's Travels

```
A W P A P H O S
S T A E F Q I U
S Y T P R L Z T
O R A A O G M E
S E R P L Y A L
E H A G R I U I
K E L A T L A M
N O D I S T O R
```

PATARA	PAPHOS	TYRE
PERGA	MILETUS	MALTA
SIDON	ATTALIA	ASSOS
MYRA	NEAPOLIS	

H

In a Bible Kitchen

```
B O W L S A L T
R V E F I N K N
O E L B A T R E
T N F B R O O M
H S A U C E F E
S X O S U A L A
I L L I P W K L
F P C K L I M E
```

FLOUR	FISH	CUP	CAKE
SAUCE	MEAL	OIL	SALT
BROOM	LOAF	MILK	KNIFE
FORK	TABLE	OVEN	BOWL
BROTH	CORN		

35. CROSSWORD

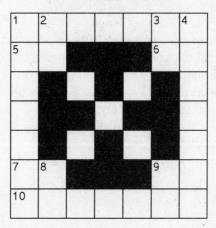

1. Across: Twice in Matthew 5:22
   Down: "He will . . . like a lily" (Hos. 14:5)
   Diagonally: Spoke proudly
2. Down: Half the Italian capital
3. Down: Double vowel
4. Down: An ephah of this sort of grain (1 Sam. 17:17)
5. Across: Behold
6. Across: Center of light
7. Across: Double nothing
8. Down: Cereal without end
9. Across: as 3 down
   Down: Printer's measure
10. Diagonally: Leviathan (Ps. 74:14)
    Across: Who "will see God's salvation" (Luke 3:6)

36. HIDDEN BIBLE TREES

FIND the Bible trees hidden in the sentences below.

1. A debtor will owe an amount of money.
2. Never was Nero a king of Israel.
3. Moses was the principal man in the exodus from Egypt.
4. The jailor in Philippi nearly lost Paul and Silas.
5. A man's mishap pleases none of his friends.
6. I cannot be forgiven if I refuse to give up wrongdoing.
7. Let us live in God's plan every day.
8. Wickedness at once darkens the light of life.
9. King Neco lived in Egypt.
10. The pilgrim waved a palm on David's city road.

37. CROSSWORD

Across

1. Zedekiah's soldiers deserted him near this place (2 Kings 25:5)
8. Friendly island kingdom
10. Come over to . . . and help us (Acts 16:9)
11. Negative
12. Saintly street
16. This official helped Philip on the Gaza road (Acts 8:27)
19. Best thing to do with a sacrifice
20. They beat the servant (Luke 20:10)

Down

2. Engrave
3. Small deer
4. Discoverer without head or tail
5. Twisted wheel tooth
6. Peter helped a lame man up with this (Acts 3:7)
7. Corrected
9. Where a road divides
13. Worn on a foot
14. Couch
15. In Tyre gold was as common as this (Zech. 9:3)
17. Twisted flipper
18. Isaiah wrote with an ordinary one (Isa. 8:1)

38. THE ARMOR OF GOD

ONE word is filled in to help. All other words can be found in Ephesians 6:13–17.

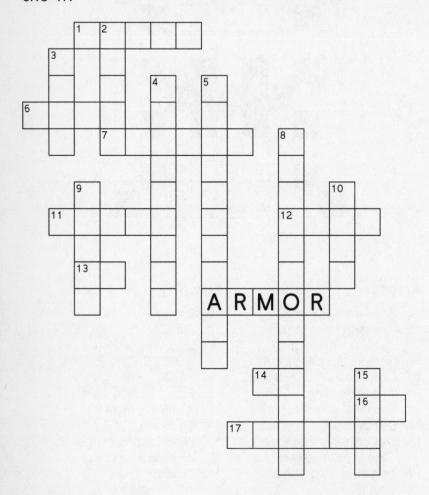

39. ANOTHER HOW MANY

WRITE the figure in the space provided at the end of the question. If you add up the column from 2 to 11 you will find the total to be the answer to the first question.

1. How many pigs drowned in the Sea of Galilee? (Mark 5:13)   -----------------

2. How many people were on board Paul's ship? (Acts 27:37)   -----------------

3. How many elders worshiped God? (Rev. 19:4)   -----------------

4. After how many years did Paul go up to Jerusalem? (Gal. 1:18)   -----------------

5. Of how many rulers was Ishmael the father? (Gen. 17:20)   -----------------

6. At what age did Amaziah become king? (2 Chron. 25:1)   -----------------

7. How many silver coins did Judas Iscariot give to the chief priests? (Matt. 26:15)   -----------------

8. In the Lord's sight, how many years are as one day? (2 Peter 3:8)   -----------------

9. How old was Noah when the flood came? (Gen. 7:6)   -----------------

10. How many men did Jesus heal? (Luke 17:12)   -----------------

11. How many servants did Ziba have? (2 Sam. 9:10)   -----------------

40. SEE HOW THEY FLY

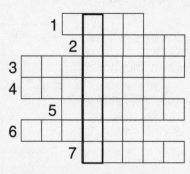

A

1. It knows when it is time to migrate. (Jer. 8:7)
2. It will hoot through the windows. (Zeph. 2:14)
3. One of the birds a Jew must not eat. (Lev. 11:16 GOOD NEWS)
4. A waterfowl with a pouch in its bill.
5. A wind brought them from the sea. (Num. 11:31)
6. Another sea bird Jews must not eat. (Deut. 14:17)
7. "Does the . . . take flight by your wisdom?" (Job 39:26)

Center column: It has "a nest for herself." (Ps. 84:3)

B

1. Symbol of the Holy Spirit (John 1:32)
2. It nests in pine trees. (Ps. 104:17)
3. They will be attracted by a dead body. (Matt. 24:28)
4. God never forgets it. (Luke 12:6)
5. A young one is suitable for sacrifice. (Lev. 1:14)
6. A bird of prey
7. A wading bird

Center column: It lays its eggs on the ground. (Job 39:14–15)

41. CROSSWORD

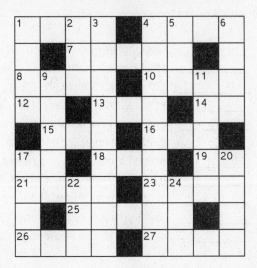

Across

1. Charge for gospel preaching (2 Cor. 11:7)
4. More than better
7. Son of Japheth (Gen. 10:2)
8. Pack
10. "The . . . has come" (Mark 1:15)
12. Negative
13. British royal abbreviation
14. Correct
15. Once Egypt (abbrev.)
16. Help
17. One
18. Fire waste
19. "And" in French
21. Prepare for publication
23. Irish
25. With Lystra (Acts 14:6)
28. Poems
27. First man

Down

1. The doe might desert it (Jer. 14:5)
2. Greek letter
3. Fourth river (Gen. 2:14)
4. Mother of Solomon (1 Kings 1:11)
5. Priest of Shiloh (1 Sam. 1:3)
6. Travel by wagon
9. Circular
11. Israel's law-giver (Exod. 19:3)
17. Air
20. Elisha's oxen
22. Fish
24. The sea dried up (Josh. 2:10)

42. BUILDING THE HOUSE

WRITE the name or word in the space provided.

1. **A** is for _____ God, builder and all (Heb. 11:10)
2. **B** for the _____ clearly seen in the wall (1 Kings 7:3)
3. **C** for the _____ holding together (Eph. 2:20)
4. **D** for the _____ which is open for ever (Rev. 3:8)
5. **E** is for _____ built platform of wood (Neh. 8:4)
6. **F** for _____ made lasting and good (1 Cor. 3:11)
7. **G** for the _____ which Haman built fine (Esther 7:9)
8. **H** is for _____ gave Solomon pine (1 Kings 5:10)
9. **I** for _____ in the temple of gold (1 Kings 6:22)
10. **J** is for _____ built by Hiel of old (1 Kings 16:34)
11. **K** is for _____ to unlock all the knowledge (Luke 11:52)
12. **L** for the _____ which left Lebanon by sea (1 Kings 5:9)
13. **M** for the _____ demolished will be (Amos 3:15)
14. **N** is for _____ the door good to enter (Luke 13:24)
15. **O** is for _____ Samaria's builder (1 Kings 16:24)
16. **P** is for _____ where the blind people lay prone (John 5:2–3)
17. **Q** for the _____ supplying the stone (1 Kings 6:7)
18. **R** is for _____ with good tiling to cover (Luke 5:19)
19. **S** is for _____ but use rock to build over (Matt. 7:26)
20. **T** is for _____ of the pine tree sort (Ezek. 27:5)
21. **U** is _____ where prayer battles were fought (Acts 1:3)
22. **V** is for _____ where houses are many (Luke 24:13)
23. **W** for _____ no place without any (Dan. 6:10)
24. **X** is for _____ who sat on a throne (Esther 2:16)
25. **Y** is for _____ blue or scarlet well sewn (Exod. 35:25)
26. **Z** is for _____ on God's holy hill (Joel 2:1)

43. ANOTHER TRIPLE COLUMN

The center three columns have the same letters and tell us what to do with good food.

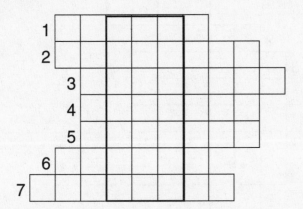

1. None in the mouths of idols (Ps. 135:17)
2. God gives food to every living one (Ps. 136:25)
3. Giant eagle had long ones (Ezek. 17:3)
4. They do not know God (1 Thess. 4:5)
5. Simon was a worker in this material (Acts 10:32)
6. Where Joab kept his sword (2 Sam. 20:8)
7. Masters must not do this to slaves (Eph. 6:9)

44. AMONG THE ARTS

EACH answer contains the word "art."

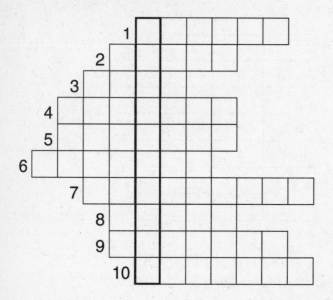

1. Trade
2. God's creation
3. Chariots do this in lightning fashion (Nah. 2:4)
4. As this Titus worked with Paul (2 Cor. 8:23)
5. An art of silver or gold (2 Kings 12:13)
6. A goddess of Ephesus (Acts 19:24)
7. The art where the king was sitting (Jer. 36:22)
8. The art on which to write (Prov. 3:3)
9. A wailing will go up from the new one (Zeph. 1:10)
10. "Terrors . . . him on every side" (Job 18:11)

Center column: Blind man of Jericho (Mark 10:46)

45. CROSSWORD

Across

1. City where the walls collapsed (Josh. 6:20)
8. Town which received David's loot (1 Sam. 30:29)
10. Gideon's son (Judg. 8:31)
11. Preposition
12. Where Haran died (Gen. 11:28)
16. I . . . to you our sister Phoebe (Rom. 16:1 GOOD NEWS)
19. Doctrine of Arius
20. Also means Syrian

Down

2. Boy's name
3. Abraham saw one caught in a bush (Gen. 22:13)
4. Made cold and solid
5. Western state (abbrev.)
6. Mixed up place of punishment
7. "Can anyone . . . him by the eyes" (Job 40:24)
9. Acting word game
13. Mark after a wound
14. Giants of Ar (Deut. 2:9 or 29 GOOD NEWS)
15. Again but reversed
17. Half a fruit
18. First part of a life jacket

ANSWERS

1. CROSSWORD

Across:

1. Lies	12. El	17. We	25. Borne
4. Rome	13. Vie(w)	18. Tot	26. Town
7. Taken	14. Sa	19. Og	27. Tame
8. Baal	15. Ova	21. Esli	
10. Poor	16. Nun	23. Aswa(n)	

Down:

1. Lobe	4. Repentant	9. Aloes	20. Gate
2. Eta	5. Ono	11. O snow	22. Lbw
3. Salvation	6. Ezra	17. West	24. Sea

2. AN ALPHABET OF HUSBANDS AND WIVES

1. Ananias	8. Hannah	15. Othniel	22. Vashti
2. Bernice	9. Isaac	16. Priscilla	23. Woman
3. Caleb	10. Joanna	17. Queen	24. Xerxes
4. David	11. Kin	18. Ruth	25. Younger
5. Eve	12. Lappidoth	19. Sarai	26. Zechariah
6. Felix	13. Milcah	20. Taphath	
7. Gomer	14. Nabal	21. Uriah	

3. WORKERS WITH PAUL

1. Eubulus	5. Priscilla	9. Trophimus
2. Archippus	6. Claudia	10. Onesiphorus
3. Tychicus	7. Aristarchus	
4. Onesimus	8. Erastus	

4. PSALM FIFTEEN

1. Fear	6. Righteous	11. His	16. Blameless
2. Never	7. Honors	12. Hurts	17. Shaken
3. Is	8. Money	13. Live	
4. Slur	9. Not	14. Usury	
5. Lends	10. Tongue	15. Oath	

5. EIGHT DAYS OF WONDER

1. Joshua   3. Deaf   5. Moses   7. New
2. Unholy   4. Great   6. Every   8. Third

Initial column: Judgment

6. REGROUP THE LETTERS

1. Romans 10:13   4. Psalm 34:8   7. Philippians 4:13
2. Romans 6:23   5. Matthew 9:37
3. Psalm 51:1   6. 1 Timothy 1:15

7. ALONG THE ROAD

1. Broad   5. Holiness   9. Shur
2. Nowadays   6. Same   10. Bashan
3. Ephrath   7. Cloaks
4. Another   8. Shechem

Center Column: Bartimaeus

8. PUT ME RIGHT

1. Live = lead   4. Oaks = oars   7. Men = him
2. Bar = jar   5. Patches = paths
3. Nests = nets   6. Prefer = prepare

9. CROSSWORD

Across:

1. Jericho   11. Mar   16. Ago   21. Us   25. Ga
7. To   12. Ma   17. Boa   22. Via   27. Servant
8. Oa(t)   13. Be   18. Go   23. CH
10. Am   14. NE   20. So   24. Me

Down:

2. Et   5. Ha   13. Bog   20. Saga
3. Rome   6. Lazarus   15. (N)ebo   24. Me
4. Corn   9. Malachi   19. Over   26. An

10. WHO ARE WE?

A Mountain   **B** Pharisee   **C** Disciple   **D** Rehoboam

11. TRIPLE COLUMN

1. Nineveh
2. Prevent
3. Reveal
4. Revenge
5. Revenue
6. Severe
7. Seven

12. HOW MANY?

1. 1,000
2. 105
3. 400
4. 2
5. 2
6. 41
7. 8
8. 40
9. 12
10. 70
11. 20
12. 300

13. AGES PAST AND PRESENT

1. Damage
2. Image
3. Savage
4. Carriage
5. Outrageous
6. Unbandage
7. Rage
8. Advantage
9. Gage
10. Eagerness
11. Dowager

Initial letters: Discouraged

14. ON THE FARM

1. Barley
2. Plowshares
3. Locusts
4. Winnowing
5. Fodder
6. Mustard
7. Harvest
8. Vineyard

Center column: Boundary

15. MINI-CROSSWORDS

A Across
1. Best
3. Tent
5. Go
6. Comb
8. Ahaz
10. Sandal
12. Am
13. Term

Down
1. Bath
2. Song
4. Tomb
6. Cast
7. Mind
8. Axle
9. Adam
11. (H)at

B Across

1. Jude	5. No	8. Ripe	12. Og
3. Horn	6. Gath	10. Darius	13. Peal

Down

1. John	4. Noah	7. Tyre	9. Pool
2. Darn	6. Gadi	8. Rose	11. Up

C Across

1. Colt	5. Ex	8. Abel	12. Is
3. Iddo	6. Turn	10. Rabbah	13. Mean

Down

1. Crib	4. Oxen	7. Robe	9. Erin
2. Lode	6. Turk	8. Ache	11. (H)am

16. CHANGING LETTERS

A	B	C	D
TAME	WORK	SEEK	COME
TIME	WORT	SEED	CORE
TILE	WERT	SEND	CARE
WILE	WEST	FEND	CART
WILD	REST	FIND	PART

17. AN ALPHABET OF BIBLE MEN

1. Abel	8. Hilkiah	15. Omri	22. Vophsi
2. Balaam	9. Isaac	16. Pilate	23. Well
3. Caleb	10. Jacob	17. Quartus	24. Xerxes
4. Demas	11. Korah	18. Rufus	25. Yoke
5. Ehud	12. Laban	19. Stephen	26. Ziba
6. Festus	13. Methuselah	20. Thomas	
7. Gamaliel	14. Naaman	21. Uzziah	

18. HIDDEN BIBLE GEMS

1. Agate	4. Pearl	6. Coral	8. Jasper
2. Topaz	5. Crystal	7. Amethyst	9. Diamond
3. Ruby			

19. PSALM TWENTY-FOUR

1. Waters	3. Lift	8. Ascend	13. Receive
2. **Across:**	4. Swear	9. False	14. Blessing
Hill	5. Earth	10. World	15. Lords
2. **Down:**	6. What	11. Founded	16. Seek
Hands	7. Established	12. Clean	17. Seas

20. WHAT A JUMBLE!

1. Mesopotamia	5. Heliopolis	9. Zaretham
2. Babylonia	6. Eziongeber	10. Zarephath
3. Nineveh	7. Beersheba	11. Jerusalem
4. Rameses	8. Bethlehem	12. Samaria

21. JUMBLED CHURCHES

1. Ephesus	3. Pergamum	5. Sardis	7. Philadelphia
2. Smyrna	4. Thyatira	6. Laodicea	

22. BROTHERS AND SISTERS

1. Simeon	3. Esau	5. Cain	7. Mary
2. Moses	4. Miriam	6. John	8. Andrew

Center column: Issachar

23. CROSSWORD

Across:

1. Toes	12. Do	17. Sa	25. Nahum
4. Noah	13. Ado	18. Ire	26. Moan
7. Latin	14. Up	19. Pi	27. Sure
8. Elim	15. Tar	21. Knit	
10. Cell	16. Dim	23. Mess	

Down:

1. Tied	4. Nicodemus	9. Lotan	20. Isle
2. Eli	5. One	11. Lumps	22. Ina
3. Samaritan	6. Help	17. Skim	24. Emu

24. ONE OF THREE

A

1. Gazzam	3. Nathan	5. Baal	7. Igal	9. Eliashib
2. Ophni	4. Job	6. Joanna	8. Hor	10. Gur

B

1. Uz	3. Cain	5. Salem	7. Nimrod	9. Rufus
2. Zillah	4. Habor	6. Zibeon	8. Patmos	10. Junias

C

1. Seth	3. Leah	5. Joram	7. Shebna	9. Zedekiah
2. Rabbah	4. Lud	6. Jehoiada	8. Jehizkiah	10. Shaphat

D

1. Ira	3. Azaziah	5. Besor	7. Hannah	9. Jadon
2. Sheba	4. Amnon	6. Elim	8. Jehiel	10. Dumah

25. THE LORD'S PRAYER

1. Kingdom	5. Father	9. Lead	12. Into
2. Daily	6. Hallowed	10. **Across:** Temptation	13. Done
3. Name	7. Will	10. **Down:** Today	
4. Bread	8. Debtors	11. Forgiven	

26. CROSSWORD

1. **Across:** Thunder	6. (L)eo
1. **Down:** Trumpet	7. (Dinn)er, (Supp)er
1. **Diagonally:** Tempter	8. Rr
2. He	9. **Across:** Ee
3. Ee	9. Down:(L)eo
4. Rooster	10. **Across:** Traitor
5. Re	10. **Diagonally:** Trapper

27. REGROUP MORE LETTERS

1. Matthew 5:9   4. Psalm 119:105   6. 2 Corinthians 6:2
2. John 15:13   5. Joshua 3:5   7. 1 Corinthians 16:13
3. Psalm 23:6

28. STRIP WORDS

A Eternal   **C** Affection   **E** Acknowledge
B Follower   **D** Allegiance

29. ODD ONE OUT

A
1. Electrician (not a Bible tradesman)
2. Thomas (not a Bible translator)
3. Romans (not a Gospel)
4. Athens (not a town in Israel)
5. Mary (not a Bible man)
6. Galilee (not a river)
7. Timothy (not an apostle)
8. Jude (not an Old Testament book)
9. Cornelius (not an Old Testament man)
10. Televise (not a Bible word)

B
1. Saul (not a prophet)
2. Ezekiel (not a king)
3. Martha (not a relative of Timothy)
4. Philistines (not a tribe of Israel)
5. Germany (not a Bible country)
6. French (not a Bible language)
7. Lost feather (not a parable)
8. Wisdom (not in 1 Corinthians 13:13)
9. Silver (not a gift brought to baby Jesus)
10. New Year (not a Christian holiday)

30. SIX-LETTER WORDS

A

1. Dorcas	3. Locust	5. Exodus
2. Samuel	4. Temple	6. Sacred

B

1. Israel	3. Elijah	5. Naaman
2. Levite	4. Heaven	6. Naggai

C

1. Sardis	3. Athens	5. Eunice
2. Smyrna	4. Salome	6. Elders

D

1. Romans	3. Naboth	5. Repent
2. Simeon	4. Helper	6. Temper

E

1. Demons	3. Martha	5. Wreath
2. Siloam	4. Andrew	6. Hatred

F

1. Hebron	3. Yonder	5. Lystra
2. Nobody	4. Repeal	6. Ahijah

31. LOST WORDS

God is our refuge and strength, an ever-present help in trouble (Ps. 46:1)

1. Rom. 8:28	5. John 15:1	9. Gal. 1:3
2. 1 John 1:5	6. Isa. 40:29	10. Ps. 40:17
3. Ps. 95:7	7. Rom. 14:12	11. 1 Cor. 13:6
4. Ps. 91:2	8. Heb. 13:8	12. Ps. 59:17

32. A COLLECTION OF ACTS

1. Phylacteries	3. Attractive	5. Tact	7. Contract
2. Reactor	4. Cactus	6. Intact	8. Exact

Initial letters: Practice

33. BY THE WATER

1. Malta	5. Nets	8. Charcoal	11. Crete
2. Fisherman	6. Seleucia	9. Boat	12. Leviathan
3. Sand	7. Oars	10. Jonah	13. Winds
4. Galilee			

Center column: Mediterranean

34. IN ALL DIRECTIONS

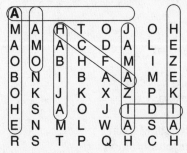

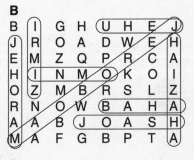

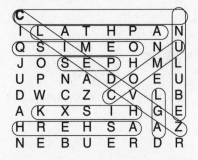

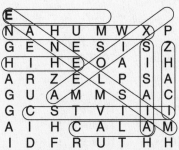

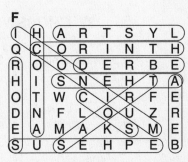

G

H
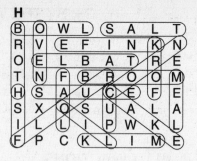

35. CROSSWORD

1. **Across:** Brother
1. **Down:** Blossom
1. **Diagonally:** Boasted
2. Ro(me)
3. Ee
4. Roasted
5. Lo

6. (N)eo(n)
7. Oo
8. Oa(t)
9. **Across:** Ee
9. **Down:** En
10. **Across:** Mankind
10. **Diagonally:** Monster

36. HIDDEN BIBLE TREES

1. Willow
2. Oak
3. Palm
4. Pine
5. Apple
6. Fir
7. Plane
8. Cedar
9. Olive
10. Almond

37. CROSSWORD

Across:

1. Jericho
8. Tonga
10. Macedonia
11. No
12. St
16. Ethiopian
19. Offer
20. Tenants

Down:

2. Etch
3. Roe
4. (F)inde(r)
5. Cgo (Cog)
6. Hand
7. Amended
9. Parting
13. Shoe
14. Sofa
15. Dirt
17. Ifn (Fin)
18. Pen

38. THE ARMOR OF GOD

1. Stand	6. Belt	10. Evil	14. In
2. Truth	7. Helmet	11. Waist	15. Able
3. Then	8. Righteousness	12. Have	16. Be
4. Salvation	9. Faith	13. To	17. Gospel
5. Breastplate			

39. ANOTHER HOW MANY

1. 2,000	3. 24	5. 12	7. 30	9. 600	11. 20
2. 276	4. 3	6. 25	8. 1,000	10. 10	

40. SEE HOW THEY FLY

A

1. Thrush	3. Seagull	5. Quails	7. Hawk
2. Owl	4. Pelican	6. Cormorant	

Center column: Swallow

B

1. Dove	3. Vultures	5. Pigeon	7. Heron
2. Stork	4. Sparrow	6. Falcon	

Center column: Ostrich

41. CROSSWORD

Across:

1. Free	12. No	17. An	23. Erse
4. Best	13. HRH	18. Ash	25. Derbe
7. Tubal	14. OK	19. Et	26. Odes
8. Wrap	15. UAR	21. Edit	27. Adam
10. Time	16. SOS		

Down:

1. Fawn	4. Bathsheba	9. Round	20. Team
2. Eta	5. Eli	11. Moses	22. Ide
3. Euphrates	6. Trek	17. Aero	24. Red

42. BUILDING THE HOUSE

1. Architect
2. Beams
3. Cornerstone
4. Door
5. Ezra
6. Foundation
7. Gallows
8. Hiram
9. Interior
10. Jericho
11. Key
12. Logs
13. Mansions
14. Narrow
15. Omri
16. Pool
17. Quarry
18. Roof
19. Sand
20. Timbers
21. Upstairs
22. Villages
23. Window
24. Xerxes
25. Yarn
26. Zion

43. ANOTHER TRIPLE COLUMN

1. Breath
2. Creature
3. Feathers
4. Heathen
5. Leather
6. Sheath
7. Threaten

44. AMONG THE ARTS

1. Barter
2. Earth
3. Dart
4. Partner
5. Article
6. Artemis
7. Apartment
8. Heart
9. Quarter
10. Startle

Center column: Bartimaeus

45. CROSSWORD

Across:
1. Jericho
8. Racal
10. Abimelech
11. To
12. Ur
16. Recommend
19. Arian
20. Aramean

Down:
2. Eric
3. Ram
4. Iced
5. Cal
6. Hlel (Hell)
7. Capture
9. Charade
13. Scar
14. Emim
15. Wena (Anew)
17. Ora(nge)
18. Mae (West)

1. BIBLE DREAMS

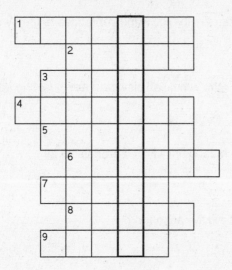

1. He dreamed of cows and corn (Gen. 41:1–7)
2. An Aramean who was warned, "Be careful" (Gen. 31:24)
3. These men were warned not to return to Herod (Matt. 2:12)
4. He dreamed in Gibeon (1 Kings 3:5)
5. He told his dream to his brothers (Gen. 37:5)
6. His wife suffered in a dream (Matt. 27:19)
7. A dream comes when there are many (Eccles. 5:3)
8. He dreamed of a stairway in Bethel (Gen. 28:12)
9. Usual time for dreams (Job 33:15)

Center column: A dreaming king of Gerar (Gen. 20:3)

2. REGROUP THE LETTERS

REGROUP the letters in the following sentences to form well-known Bible verses.

1. Ol ordo urlo rdho wmaj esti cisy ourn amei nal lthe ear th.

2. Whoe verco mest omei wil lnev erdri veaw ay.

3. Li vein pea cewi the acho the r.

4. Mys hiel disgo dmos thig hwh osa vest heu prig hti nhe art.

5. Go dlin esswi thcon tent men tisg rea tga in.

6. Thel or dgiv esst ren gtht ohi spe ople.

7. Ca stal lyo uran xie tyon hi mbec aus ehec are sfo ryou.

3. SAME FOR THREE

ADD the same word before each word in a line to make yet another word; for example, laid, power, and run can be preceded by "over." All words appear in the NIV.

1. some, breadth, ful
2. prints, hills, steps
3. spring, set, shoots
4. fearing, less, liness
5. man, dom, will
6. ager, made, kind
7. examined, bar, roads
8. keeper, post, way
9. grade, born, way
10. flowing, lasting, more

4. EIGHT BIBLE GATES

THE answers to these "gate" questions appear in alphabetical order.

1. _____ In what cave was David hiding when he asked for water from the well at the gate of Bethlehem? (2 Sam. 23:13)

2. _____ Who sat at a town gate and bought some land from Naomi? (Ruth 4:1, 9)

3. _____ What sort of man was healed at the Beautiful Gate in Jerusalem? (Acts 3:2)

4. _____ What gate did the Lord threaten to break down? (Amos 1:5)

5. _____ What men sat as judges at the town gate? (Deut. 21:19)

6. _____ What gates of heaven has God promised to open to pour out a blessing? (Mal. 3:10)

7. _____ At what gate did the second choir stop in the City of David in Nehemiah's day? (Neh. 12:39)

8. _____ Above which gate did each priest make repairs in front of his own house? (Neh. 3:28)

5. IN ALL DIRECTIONS

THE words appear forward, backward, upward, downward, or diagonally. Circle each word.

Nine Apostles

A.

```
S   A   M   O   H   T   A   Z
N   C   N   O   M   I   S   P
N   S   A   D   U   J   O   H
O   B   P   Q   R   J   G   I
J   D   E   C   D   Y   O   L
M   A   T   T   H   E   W   I
W   A   E   M   A   J   V   P
H   M   R   I   K   S   N   C
```

Twelve Nouns in Psalm 1

B.

```
A   D   E   L   I   G   H   T
T   S   E   A   S   O   N   R
H   T   S   D   N   I   W   E
G   R   R   E   T   A   W   E
I   E   Z   K   M   B   D   S
N   A   M   C   W   B   E   W
K   M   C   I   O   A   L   A
Q   S   N   W   T   P   L   Y
```

Eleven Herbs, Plants, and Vegetables

C.

```
R   E   B   M   U   C   U   C
M   O   E   Q   E   C   Z   U
A   I   A   M   T   I   P   M
L   E   N   T   I   L   O   M
O   K   A   T   L   R   S   I
E   K   R   I   C   A   S   N
K   E   D   A   M   G   Y   B
N   L   M   Y   R   R   H   L
```

Twelve Tools and Implements

D.

```
C   Z   D   R   E   F   W   K
A   H   R   H   S   W   P   N
N   T   I   N   A   I   L   I
P   J   B   S   K   R   O   F
H   A   M   M   E   R   U   E
M   P   X   Q   H   L   G   C
A   W   L   E   V   O   H   S
T   S   I   C   K   L   E   J
```

6. WHO ARE WE?

A.   My first is in PETER but never in JOHN
My next's not in DULLNESS but clearly in SHONE
My third is in EVIL but misses the GOOD
My next is in CHISEL but not in the WOOD
My fifth is in EGYPT as well as the NILE
My sixth's in AMUSE but not in REVILE
My next's found in JORDAN and in KISHON too
My last is in ANCIENT as well as in NEW
                    My whole's a New Testament letter

B.   My first is in WOMAN as well as in MAN
My next's seen in WALKING, in STANDING, and RAN
My third is in TEACHING but never in LEARN
My fourth's in STRAIGHT as well as in TURN
My next is in HEAVY and also in LIGHT
My sixth's in the DAYTIME and shines in the NIGHT
My next is in ABRAM but never in LOT
My last is in SLEEPER but not in the COT
                    My whole took the place of Judas

C.   My first is in MATTHEW but missing in LUKE
My next comes in CHALLENGE but not in REBUKE
My third's not in LIFE or in TRUTH but in WAY
My fourth's not in SEEKING but there when we PRAY
My next is in MALTA but never in ROME
My sixth comes in LODGINGS although not in HOME
My next's seen in NEAR and stands clearly in FAR
My last is in HEAVEN and in judgment BAR
                    My whole is the home of Lydia

D.   My first is in BABEL and in BABYLON
My next's not in COMING but clearly in GONE
In CAIN lies my third one, in EDEN and NOD
My fourth comes in JACOB but not in NIMROD
Both HEAVEN and HAPPY contain my next sign
While YOURS has no next line but stands out in MINE
My sixth is in VILLAGE but not in a TOWN
My last's not in CROSS but shines in the CROWN
                    My whole is a son of Jacob

7. LET'S GO TO WORK

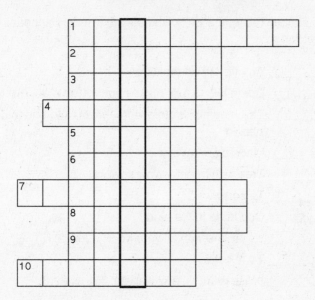

1. They took forty days to prepare Jacob's body (Gen. 50:3)
2. He cleanses cloth (Mark 9:3 KJV)
3. Maker of linen and cloth
4. Israelites were expected to gather straw to make them (Exod. 5:7)
5. He makes bread
6. They worked with carpenters and builders (2 Kings 22:6)
7. Paul as a tradesman (Acts 18:3)
8. She grasps it with her fingers (Prov. 31:19)
9. Worker in clay
10. A tax-collector (Matt. 10:3)

Center column: Not one could be found in Israel (1 Sam. 13:19)

8. TEN FULL URNS

ALL answers contain the letters URN, and the initial letters appear in alphabetical order.

1. _____ An offering on the altar

2. _____ Doing this to milk makes butter (Prov. 30:33)

3. _____ Three administrators were thrown into one that blazed

4. _____ Made by a traveler

5. _____ Tree with bright yellow flowers

6. _____ To sorrow

7. _____ Occurring in the night

8. _____ ". . . to me with all your heart" (Joel 2:12)

9. _____ To reject

10. _____ "Wise men . . . away anger" (Prov. 29:8)

9. JUMBLED COUNTRIES

UNJUMBLE the following lines to find ten biblical cities.

1. I SPARE
2. SCRUPY
3. PEGTY
4. GRAY HIP
5. HAPPY MAIL
6. I CON A DAME
7. OH I ATE PI
8. AS RAY IS
9. ERECT
10. PAC A PAID CO

10. SAILING AWAY

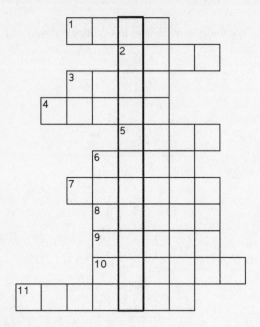

1. Jesus crossed the lake in one
2. Jonah slept below . . . (Jonah 1:5)
3. Used to row a boat
4. He traveled inside a great fish
5. Made from a cedar from Lebanon (Ezek. 27:5)
6. Seaside town near Sidon (Matt. 15:21)
7. "Ships coming from the shores of . . ." (Num. 24:24)
8. It is a danger to shipping
9. A centurion unwisely followed his advice (Acts 27:11)
10. Used to steer a ship (James 3:4)
11. He built ships at Ezion Geber (1 Kings 9:26)

Center column: Paul borrowed a ship from this Mysian city
   (Acts 27:2)

11. LOST WORDS

FILL in the missing words. A well-known Bible verse will appear as you read them downwards.

1. _____ to the LORD and his strength (Ps. 105:4)

2. For _____ LORD is good and his love endures forever (Ps. 100:5)

3. Worthy is the _____ who was slain (Rev. 5:12)

4. I am the bread _____ life (John 6:35)

5. We believe and know that you are the Holy One of _____ (John 6:68)

6. _____ shall separate us from the love of Christ? (Rom. 8:35)

7. Blessed is the man who _____ refuge in him (Ps. 34:8)

8. He [the hired hand] abandons the sheep and runs _____ (John 10:12)

9. I am _____ gate for the sheep (John 10:7)

10. The blood of Jesus, his Son, purifies us from all _____ (1 John 1:7)

11. Jesus _____ Nazareth is passing by (Luke 18:37)

12. I am the true vine, and my Father is _____ gardener (John 15:1)

13. God so loved the _____ that he gave his one and only Son (John 3:16)

12. PYRAMIDS

FORM word pyramids using the clues. Each line uses the rearranged letters of the previous line plus an additional letter.

A.

1. Vowel
2. In the same degree
3. Mediterranean is one
4. Brother of Jacob (Gen. 25:25–26)
5. Relish or condiment
6. "A stone that . . . men to stumble"

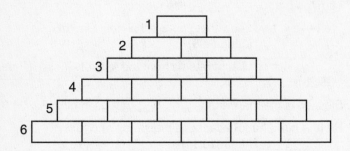

B.

1. Vowel
2. In the direction of
3. Negative
4. Heavy weights
5. Goliath was killed with one (1 Sam. 17:49)
6. Always give this type of answer

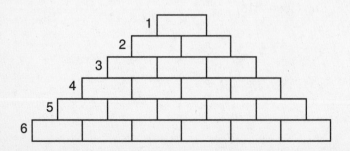

13. LIMERICKS

ADD the missing words to complete the following limericks.

A.   There was once a poor widow in _____
     Whose son died in terrible pain;
          Then Jesus drew near,
          Said: "Be of good_____;
     I'll make the young boy live again!"

B.   When on the mount _____ met multitudes
     He never addressed them in platitudes;
          He spoke to them clearly,
          For he loved them all dearly,
     And gave them eight helpful _____.

C.   With _____ Paul went to _____,
     Where in preaching he was a persister;
          To us it seems odd
          People thought him a god—
     He was just like a brother or sister.

D.   Paul wandered through _____ great city
     And thought what he saw such a pity:
          An _____ of stone
          To a god they'd not known;
     Of the true God he told the committee.

14. CHANGING LETTERS

CHANGE one letter at a time to find a connected word.

A.   C   O   R   N

—   —   —   —   Early part of the day

—   —   —   —   Sound of an owl (Mic. 1:8)

—   —   —   —   Lend

—   —   —   —   Disciples had only one in
their boat (Mark 8:14)

B.   G   A   I   N

—   —   —   —   Abel's brother

—   —   —   —   Woman found a lost one
(Luke 15:9)

—   —   —   —   Sort of cloth

—   —   —   —   Timothy's grandmother (2 Tim. 1:5)

—   —   —   —   What was once "profit I now
consider . . ." for the sake of
Christ (Phil. 3:8)

C.   C   O   L   D

—   —   —   —   "Take . . . of the eternal life"
(1 Tim. 6:12)

—   —   —   —   Past tense of above

—   —   —   —   Not to swear by this (Matt. 5:36)

—   —   —   —   Produced by the sun

15. REGROUP MORE LETTERS

REGROUP the following letters to form well-known Bible verses.

1. Liv eal ifeo flo veju stasc hri stlo vedu sand gav ehims elf upfo rus.

2. Thel or dism yst reng than dmys hi eld.

3. The refo reas weh aveop port uni tyle tus dogo odtoa llpeople.

4. B less edi sthem anw homg odcor rects.

5. B utse ekfir sthi skin gdo man dhi srig hteo usn ess.

6. Thep ray ero far igh teo usma nisp owe rfula ndef fect ive.

7. T helo rdism ylighta ndm ysa lvat ion.

16. NAMES AND PLACES

FILL in the squares according to the corresponding clues. Then discover places visited by Paul by writing the numbered letters in the second grid.

A		4	30				
B	2						
C	6						
D		15					5
E			33	10			
F	40						
G		1			19		
H		28					
I	36	27		43			
J			12	25			
K		38	21				
L			9	26	7		
M		24					
N			11				
O			17				
P			31	41			
Q	37		22	14			
R			32				
S		3			20		
T			16				

A. The first man (Gen. 2:20)
B. Town of confusion (Gen. 11:9)
C. The Promised Land
  (Deut. 32:49)
D. Large crowds from here
  followed Jesus (Matt. 4:25)
E. Land of corn
F. Governor in Caesarea
  (Acts 23:24)
G. Threshed wheat in a
  winepress (Judg. 6:11)
H. King of Judea (Luke 1:5)
I. Prophet in days of Ahaz
  (Isa. 1:1)
J. Son of Noah (Gen. 6:10)
K. Father of Saul (1 Sam. 9:3)
L. Rose from the dead
  (John 12:1)

M. Paul passed here on the way
  to Troas (Acts 16:8)
N. Ark builder (Gen. 6:14)
O. Land of gold (1 Kings 9:28)
P. Also called Simon (Matt. 4:18)
Q. Desert birds (Exod. 16:13)
R. Daughter of Bethuel
  (Gen. 22:23)
S. Traveler who helped injured
  man (Luke 10:33)
T. Received two letters from Paul
U. Hittite in David's army
  (2 Sam. 11:3)
V. Grape garden
W. One lived in Nain (Luke 7:12)
X. King of Persia (Esther 1:1)
Y. Color
Z. Father of James and John
  (Matt. 4:21)

17. A BIBLE WARDROBE

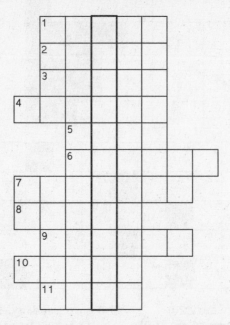

1. General word for clothing and worn with sandals (Ezek. 16:10)
2. Gives hair for clothing (Matt. 3:4)
3. Fragrant with myrrh, aloes, and cassia (Ps. 45:8)
4. Women of Zion wore them as ornaments (Isa. 3:20)
5. A wife selects it with flax (Prov. 31:13)
6. Women of Zion wore these on their heads (Isa. 3:23)
7. Worn on the apostles' feet (Mark 6:9)
8. Another word for cloaks (Isa. 3:22)
9. A rich man dressed in this and lived in luxury (Luke 16:19)
10. Mordecai wore a robe of this material (Esther 8:15)
11. More valuable than clothes (Luke 12:23)

Center column: A princess wears this type of garment when led to the king (Ps. 45:14)

18. ADD THE FIGURES

IN the space provided write the number that completes the phrase. Add up the column for the final answer.

1. _____ tribes of Israel

2. _____ God and Father of mankind

3. _____ days and nights of rain when Noah was in the ark (Gen. 7:12)

4. _____ epistles to Timothy

5. _____ persons in the Godhead

6. _____ Beatitudes (Matt. 5:3–10)

7. _____ smooth stones of David (1 Sam. 17:40)

8. _____ days of creation

9. _____ ungrateful lepers healed by Jesus (Luke 17:17)

10. _____ silver coins given to Judas (Matt. 26:15)

11. _____ gospels

12. _____ Commandments

Total: _____ The age Jacob claimed to be as he spoke to Pharaoh (Gen. 47:9)

19. IN THE DESERT

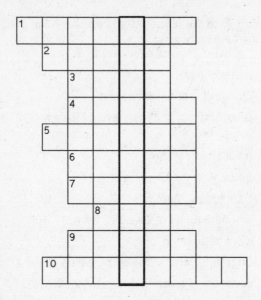

1. What Isaiah said will be in the desert (Isa. 35:8)
2. Brought in by a wind from the sea (Num. 11:31)
3. Aaron made it out of gold (Exod. 32:4)
4. John preached in the Desert of . . . (Matt. 3:1)
5. "The LORD shakes the Desert of . . ." (Ps. 29:8)
6. His men were lost in a desert earthquake (Num. 16:32)
7. The Israelites' main desert diet (Exod. 16:31)
8. This sea divided to help the Israelites (Exod. 15:4)
9. He tended Jethro's sheep on "the far side of the desert" (Exod. 3:1)
10. First commemorated by the Israelites in the desert (Lev. 23:5)

Center column: Another name for desert

20. MINI-CROSSWORDS

A.

B.

ACROSS

1. Strike
3. Human being
5. Often goes with drank
7. Engraving is one (2 Chron. 2:7)
9. Omega (Rev. 21:6)
10. Every
11. Babylon's . . . will be silenced (Jer. 51:55)

DOWN

1. Son of Noah (Gen. 6:10)
2. Number of commandments
4. The sluggard must take it as an example (Prov. 6:6)
5. Girl's name
6. Fish
7. "Let the wise listen and . . . to their learning" (Prov. 1:5)
8. Metal (Num. 31:22)

ACROSS

1. Color
3. Carried by a shepherd
5. Before "jamin" and "hadad" (Gen. 35:18; 1 Kings 15:18)
7. Witnessed
9. Tree
10. Conflict
11. Japanese coin

DOWN

1. Coated Moses' basket (Exod. 2:3)
2. Land of Cain (Gen. 4:16)
4. Number of real gods
5. Goes with arrow
6. Neither
7. The expanse (Gen. 1:8)
8. Gain victory

21. STRIP WORDS

A main word fills each strip and can be built up by answering the two or three clues for each puzzle, placing the letters in the numbered squares.

A.

1	2	3	4	5	6	7

Main word (1–7): land known for its cedars
1, 4, 7, 2: country road; 5, 6, 3: home of Ahimelech the priest (1 Sam. 21:1)

B.

1	2	3	4	5	6	7	8

Main word (1–8): Sicilian port visited by Paul
5, 3, 2: "At midnight the . . . rang out"; 7, 8, 4: a body of water; 6, 1: you and me

C.

1	2	3	4	5	6	7	8	9

Main word (1–9): town on the Sea of Galilee
3, 2, 1, 4: step; 8, 5: Abraham's birthplace; 9, 7, 6: God's greatest creation

D.

1	2	3	4	5	6	7	8	9	10

Main word (1–10): Aegean Sea island visited by Paul
5, 4: preposition; 7, 2, 3: Abraham saw one in a thicket; 9, 6, 8, 1, 10: "Will you . . . after dry chaff?" (Job 13:25)

E.

1	2	3	4	5	6	7	8	9	10	11

Main word (1–11): residents of this land visited Jerusalem at Pentecost
4: round letter; 5, 2, 11: small vegetable; 8, 10, 1: ". . . for perfection" (2 Cor. 13:11); 9, 6, 3, 7: majority

F.

1	2	3	4	5	6	7	8	9	10	11	12

Main word (1–12): one of the seven churches in the Revelation
2, 12, 3, 8: plague in Egypt; 9, 5, 11, 6: account settled; 10, 7, 4, 1: it comes from the Lord (Ps. 121:2)

22. WELLS AND SPRINGS

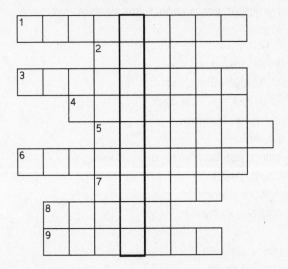

1. Where Isaac's servant dug a well (Gen. 26:33)
2. Valley made into a place of springs (Ps. 84:6)
3. David longed for water from this well (1 Chron. 11:17)
4. God causes springs to pour water into these (Ps. 104:10)
5. God turned this ground into flowing springs (Ps. 107:35)
6. This sort of man who gives way to the wicked is like a muddied spring (Prov. 25:26)
7. A well associated with Abner (2 Sam. 3:26)
8. His well was at Sychar (John 4:5)
9. Who dug the well the Israelites sang about in Beer? (Num. 21:18)

Center column: You will draw water joyfully from these wells (Isa. 12:3)

23. THINGS IN COMMON

WHAT do the names or words in each line have in common?

A.
1. Tiberias, Dead, Red
2. Omri, Jeroboam, Jehu
3. Nazareth, Capernaum, Nain
4. Lost sheep, lost son, lost coin
5. James, Andrew, Matthew
6. Dan, Levi, Asher
7. Prophesying, speaking in tongues, healing
8. Altar, lectern, belfry
9. Romans, Acts, James
10. Philip, Andrew, Peter

B.
1. Shem, Ham, Japheth
2. Gold, incense, myrrh
3. Sardis, Ephesus, Pergamum
4. Jonah, Isaiah, Noah
5. Asa, Ahaz, Ahaziah
6. Elijah, Elisha, Isaiah
7. Pishon, Gihon, Tigris
8. Zither, lyre, flute
9. Ararat, Olives, Horeb
10. Sun, moon, stars

24. PSALM FORTY-SIX

ALL words are found in Psalm 46:1–7.

HE	NOT	QUAKE	FORTRESS
IN	FOAM	RIVER	STRENGTH
IS	MOST	DWELLS	MOUNTAINS
OF	ROAR	UPROAR	
AND	EARTH	WATERS	
ARE	MELTS	ALMIGHTY	

25. MAKE THE TRIO

SUPPLY the missing word in each line to complete a well-known trio.

1. Shem, _____, Japheth
2. Gold, incense, _____
3. Morning, _____, night
4. _____, Son, Holy Ghost
5. Latin, Aramaic, _____
6. _____, Meshach, Abednego
7. Ice, snow, _____
8. _____, drink, be merry
9. Faith, hope, _____
10. Way, _____, life
11. _____, tekel, peres (Dan. 5:26)

26. HIDDEN BIBLE RIVERS

FIND the rivers hidden in the sentences below.

1. It is healthy to eat a banana for breakfast (2 Kings 5:12).
2. Would you prefer to meet a raj or Daniel (Gen. 13:10)?
3. One of the servants of Elisha borrowed an iron axe-head and let it fall into the water (2 Kings 17:6).
4. Samson broke bar and doorposts in Gaza (Ezek. 1:1).
5. The sun over Philippi shone brightly (Gen. 2:11).
6. Jubal used a cup, harp, a rod, and flutes (2 Kings 5:12).
7. There was in Kedar no nonsense with lambs and goats (Num. 21:13).
8. Swearing and stealing I honestly detest (Gen. 2:13).

27. THE FIRST PSALM

ALL words are found in Psalm 1.

MAN	WIND	DELIGHT	PROSPERS
DOES	BLOWS	MOCKERS	RIGHTEOUS
LEAF	PERISH	PLANTED	THEREFORE
SEAT	SEASON	SINNERS	
TREE	BLESSED	STREAMS	

28. THE HUNDREDTH PSALM

ALL words appear in Psalm 100.

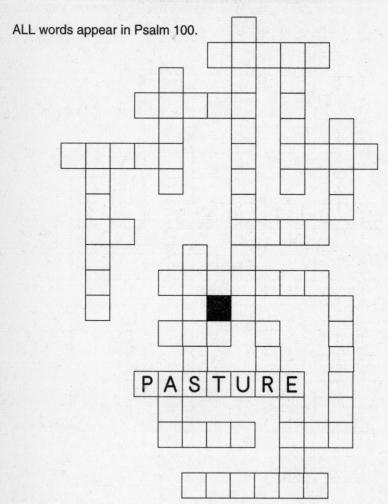

PASTURE

US			
ALL	KNOW	SERVE	PEOPLE
ARE	LOVE	SHEEP	THANKS
FOR	NAME	SHOUT	ENDURES
THE	EARTH	BEFORE	WORSHIP
GOOD	ENTER	COURTS	FAITHFULNESS

29. HELP IN TIME OF NEED

ALL answers contain the letters AID, and the initial letters appear in alphabetical order.

1. _____ An offering on the altar
1. _____ "Don't be . . ." said Jesus to Simon (Luke 5:10)
2. _____ Form of hair dress (1 Tim. 2:9)
3. _____ "The king made a great throne . . . with ivory" (1 Kings 10:18)
4. _____ Builder did this with foundations
5. _____ Servant girl
6. _____ Lost, although not forever
7. _____ Settled debt
8. _____ Joab returned from this with plunder (2 Sam 3:22)
9. _____ "God . . . , 'Let there be light'" (Gen. 1:3)
10. _____ Sober and steady

30. BIBLE PLACES

COMPLETE the name of each place by adding the first three letters.

1.	_____ AEL		11.	_____ AUS	
2.	_____ RUS		12.	_____ HOS	
3.	_____ DOD		13.	_____ BIA	
4.	_____ MEL		14.	_____ RNA	
5.	_____ DAN		15.	_____ LAG	
6.	_____ RON		16.	_____ DIS	
7.	_____ TRA		17.	_____ HAN	
8.	_____ DES		18.	_____ BOA	
9.	_____ GAH		19.	_____ ENE	
10.	_____ HAR		20.	_____ EAD	

31. BIBLE PEOPLE

COMPLETE each name by adding the first three letters.

1.	_____ UEL		11.	_____ SON	
2.	_____ MAS		12.	_____ LIP	
3.	_____ EPH		13.	_____ MER	
4.	_____ JAM		14.	_____ ANI	
5.	_____ GAI		15.	_____ IUS	
6.	_____ HER		16.	_____ BEN	
7.	_____ HUA		17.	_____ XES	
8.	_____ ECH		18.	_____ SHA	
9.	_____ ILA		19.	_____ DAD	
10.	_____ ICE		20.	_____ ATE	

32. THE TRADERS ARE COMING

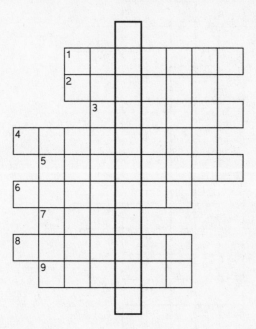

1. Joseph was sold for twenty of these (Gen. 37:28)
2. Lydia dealt in this cloth (Acts 16:14)
3. Some merchants used dishonest ones (Hosea 12:7)
4. Ships from this place carried heavy cargo (Ezek. 27:25)
5. Some turn from their routes (Job 6:18)
6. Cedar and pine logs were hauled from here to the sea (1 Kings 5:9)
7. Hiram's ships were filled with this metal (1 Kings 10:11)
8. Imported from Egypt for 600 shekels (1 Kings 10:29)
9. Solomon bought them from Egypt (1 Kings 10:28)

Center column: Jesus would not allow it to be carried through the temple (Mark 11:16)

33. OUTSPOKEN PROPHETS

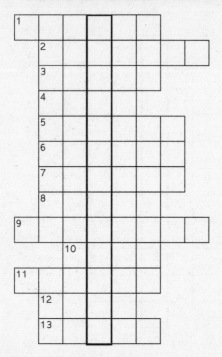

1. Tishbite associated with Mount Carmel (1 Kings 18:18–19)
2. Wrote about a valley of dry bones
3. He made a golden calf (Exod. 32:3–4)
4. He met an army as it returned to Samaria (2 Chron. 28:9)
5. Once a temple boy
6. Prophet of Shiloh (1 Kings 11:29)
7. Christian prophet who predicted a famine (Acts 11:28)
8. He wrote an oracle concerning Nineveh
9. He lived in Rehoboam's time (1 Kings 12:22)
10. He built an ark (Gen 6:13–14)
11. He told Naaman to wash in the Jordan (2 Kings 5:9)
12. An Old Testament prophet who wrote about locusts
13. Son of Beeri

Center column: (a) He wrote of a potter at work
(b) He refused to be known as the son of Pharaoh's daughter (Heb. 11:24)

34. SEVEN-LETTER WORDS

THE last letter of the first line is the same as the first letter of the next line, and so on.

A.

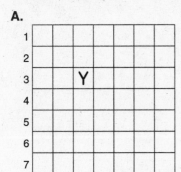

1. One of the four Gospels
2. It will be fair when the sky is red (Matt. 16:2)
3. A king's family
4. Produced
5. David prayed: ". . . me from my enemies" (Ps. 59:1)
6. We must not seek it (Lev. 19:18)
7. Father of Azor (Matt. 1:13)

B.

1. "They began to . . . against the landowner" (Matt. 20:11)
2. City of Artemis (Acts 19:35)
3. The wise king of Israel (1 Kings 4:29)
4. Naught
5. The district to which Joseph withdrew (Matt. 2:22)
6. Imperial ruler
7. Harvesting crops

C.

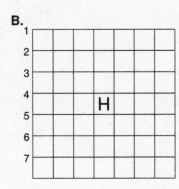

1. He "watered the seed" that Paul planted (1 Cor. 3:6)
2. Sychar was in this district (John 4:5)
3. Where the followers of Jesus were first called Christians (Acts 11:26)
4. Godless
5. Jonah was told to go to this great city (Jonah 1:2)
6. The reaping time
7. Aramaic word for "little girl" (Mark 5:41)

35. METALS AND MINERALS

WHEN all squares are filled in, the center column will reveal a pattern.

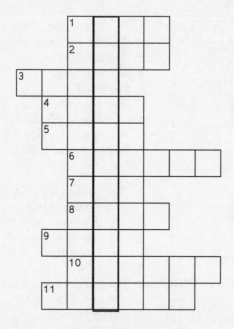

1. This spring cannot produce fresh water (James 3:11)
2. It is countless on the seashore (Heb. 11:12)
3. Mineral for washing (Jer. 2:22)
4. To be worked before repairing the brickwork (Nah. 3:14)
5. Pharaoh's army "sank like . . . in the mighty waters" (Exod. 15:10)
6. Demetrius used it to make shrines to Artemis (Acts 19:24)
7. Melted with a fiery blast (Ezek. 22:20)
8. Found in Havilah (Gen. 2:11)
9. It sharpens itself (Prov. 27:17)
10. Smelted from ore (Job 28:2)
11. Used to make mirrors (Job 37:18)

36. CROSSWORD

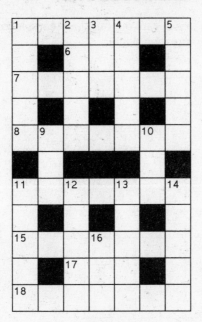

ACROSS

1. Son of David
   (2 Sam. 12:24)
6. Devour
7. Look after
8. Martha and Mary
   were . . .
11. "This is the . . . we
    have heard"
    (1 John 1:5)
15. Lines on maps
17. Father of Joshua
    (Num. 27:18)
18. Between 13 and 19
    years old

DOWN

1. People who live in Scotland
2. A vegetable eaten in Egypt
   (Num. 11:5)
3. Used for rowing
4. Mixed up meats
5. "My God will meet all your . . ."
   (Phil. 4:19)
9. "Sparkling like . . . and awesome"
   (Ezek. 1:22)
10. An old cloth
11. Damp
12. The people of Shinar used brick
    instead of this (Gen. 11:3)
13. A river in Damascus (2 Kings 5:12)
14. A girl's name
16. May be a currant one

37. PARENTS AND CHILDREN

EACH line is the name of a parent or son. Upon completion the bold squares will reveal an interesting pattern.

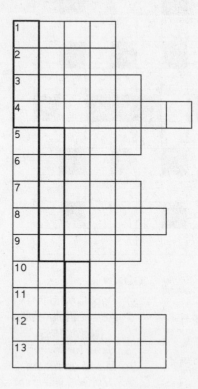

1. Father of Cain (Gen. 4:1)
2. Son of Jotham
   (2 Kings 16:1)
3. Eighth son of Jacob
   (Gen. 30:13)
4. Son of Joash (2 Kings 14:1)
5. Son of Isaac (Gen. 25:26)
6. Father of Jonathan
   (1 Sam. 14:1)
7. Son of Jephunneh
   (Num. 13:6)
8. Hannah's son (1 Sam. 1:20)
9. Son of Jesse (Ruth 4:22)
10. Father of Obed (Ruth 4:21)
11. Father of Shem (Gen. 5:32)
12. Son of Amoz (Isa. 1:1)
13. Mother of King Absalom
    (2 Sam. 3:3)

38. TWOS AND THREES

PAIR off the syllables to make twelve Bible names or places. Write the list below the grid.

A.

LTA	LA	LY	JA	JA	ETE
ER	MES	EG	JO	DE	SID
SIL	COB	ON	ITA	AS	BAN
NAH	CR	MA	RBE	YPT	PET

_____   _____   _____

_____   _____   _____

_____   _____   _____

_____   _____

B.

AS	SAM	LOE	ER	TUB	VID
AH	TI	JOA	JUD	OS	JE
OP	DA	SSE	OD	CH	TUS
ASH	AL	MAR	SH	HER	HIR

_____   _____   _____

_____   _____   _____

_____   _____   _____

_____   _____   _____

39. MORE NAMES AND PLACES

FILL in the squares according to the corresponding clues. Then discover the names of seven apostles by writing the numbered letters in the second grid.

A						
B	17					■
C			3		■	
D				10		12
E				26		■
F	6	38				
G		14	8		2	
H				13		■
I	23				■	
J (34 19 24)	15			5	■	
K		21		25		■
L	9				40	
M (42)			28			
N				11	■	
O		■	■	■	■	
P		31		.		
Q	20			4		
R		16		27		■
S		37				36
T	22		44		■	

The crossword grids with letter labels U, V, W, X, Y, Z and numbered cells.

Top grid clues / numbers:
- U
- V — 35, 39
- 18 7 33 W — 29, 32
- X
- Y — 30
- Z — 43, 1, 41

Lower grid numbered 1–44.

A. Wife of Nabal (1 Sam. 25:3)
B. Once called Luz (Gen. 28:19)
C. Paul sailed along its shore (Acts 27:12)
D. Rebekah's nurse (Gen. 35:8)
E. Elijah's successor (1 Kings 19:19)
F. Followed Felix as governor of Judea (Acts 24:27)
G. Where Saul died (1 Sam. 31:18)
H. Mountain northeast of the Jordan (Deut. 3:8)
I. Son of Abraham (Gen. 21:3)
J. Was seven when he became king (2 Kings 11:21)
K. Valley outside Jerusalem (2 Kings 23:4)
L. Lived 777 years (Gen. 5:31)
M. Last Old Testament book

N. Remembered for his vineyard (1 Kings 21:1)
O. King of Bashan (Num. 21:33)
P. Land of Cyrus (2 Chron. 36:22)
Q. Corinthian who sent greetings to Paul (Rom. 16:23)
R. People who lived in Italy's capital
S. City of refuge in Ephraim (Josh. 20:7)
T. Home of Paul (Acts 21:39)
U. Chaldean city (Gen. 11:28)
V. Queen of Xerxes (Esther 1:9)
W. Cold season
X. Father of Darius (Dan. 9:1)
Y. Another form of the name *Judah* (2 Kings 14:28)
Z. Mountain where snow fell (Ps. 68:14)

40. THE FOURTH COMMANDMENT

ALL words are found in Exodus 20:8–11.

BY	NOT	LORD	LABOR	SEVENTH
DO	SEA	MADE	SHALL	REMEMBER
OR	SIX	WORK	RESTED	DAUGHTER
TO	THE	EARTH	BLESSED	MANSERVANT
BUT	HOLY	GATES	SABBATH	

41. THREES AND FOURS

PAIR off the syllables to make twelve Bible names or places. Write the list below the grid.

A.

SAM	ANT	NIAS	SAR	ATH	CAN
EPH	DIS	DOR	SAPP	CAL	ARIA
NAZA	VARY	JOS	AAN	IOCH	SAM
ENS	HIRA	UEL	RETH	ANA	CAS

_____   _____   _____

_____   _____   _____

_____   _____   _____

_____   _____   _____

B.

LYS	ICE	JAH	ARA	TARS	GID
BIA	HANY	TUS	CYP	EUN	DAN
HISH	NAH	JOR	TRA	BET	HAN
RUS	SAL	EON	AMIS	FES	ELI

_____   _____   _____

_____   _____   _____

_____   _____   _____

_____   _____   _____

42. MORE PYRAMIDS

FORM word pyramids using the clues. Each line uses the rearranged letters of the previous line plus an additional letter.

A. 1. Vowel
    2. "And" in French
    3. Complete collection
    4. Sunday is a day of . . .
    5. Shed in sorrow
    6. Christian festival

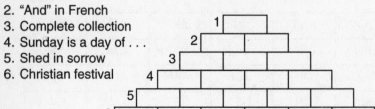

B. 1. Vowel
    2. Exists
    3. We do this in a chair
    4. Cut
    5. Steps in a wall
    6. Jesus has many—Son
       of Man is one

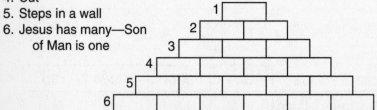

C. 1. Vowel
    2. Abraham's birthplace (Gen. 11:27–28)
    3. "They will . . . and not grow weary" (Isa. 40:31)
    4. What we do with incense
    5. Of a town or city
    6. Worn on Aaron's
       head (Exod. 29:6)

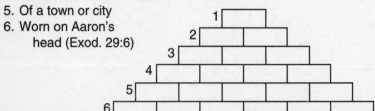

43. LAND OF EGYPT

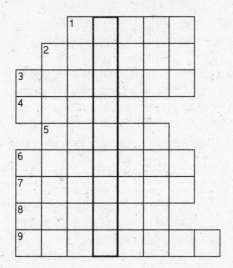

1. Israelites were expected to gather their own to make bricks (Exod. 5:7)
2. Sister of Moses (Exod. 15:20)
3. A store city in Egypt (Exod. 1:11)
4. One of Egypt's boundaries (Ezek. 29:10)
5. Became son of Pharaoh's daughter (Exod. 2:10)
6. Eighth plague in Egypt (Exod. 10:4)
7. King's title in Egypt
8. Sold and taken to Egypt (Gen. 37:28)
9. Israel's last meal before escaping from Egypt (Exod. 12:27)

Center column: ". . . of Egypt" (Heb. 11:26)

44. WHO ARE WE AGAIN?

A. My first is in BUTTER and also in BREAD
My next's not in CUTTING but clearly in SHRED
I come to the TABLE but sit not in a CHAIR
My fourth shines in CHERRY but never in PEAR
My fifth's not in PUDDING though glowing in LAMB
My sixth is in PINEAPPLE but not in the HAM
My last is in HONEY, in RYE, and in YAM

 My whole is where Jesus dined with Martha and Mary

B. My first is in JUDAS and starts JOHN as well
My second's in VALLEY and found in the DELL
My next comes in FORWARD as well as RESTRAINT
My fourth comes in SINNER as well as the SAINT
My next is in CITY but never in TOWN
My sixth sat in tree HEIGHTS but not when it's DOWN
My last is in HOME, a place of RENOWN

 My whole is where Zacchaeus was chief tax collector

C. My first is in FOUNTAIN though never in WELL
My next's found in HEAVEN but missing in HELL
My third's in a Zebra and in every ZOO
My fourth is in NOAH and in his ARK too
I'm not seen in SYNAGOGUE but heard in the PRAYER
My sixth's in my KNEELING and twice ANYWHERE
My next's in the SACRAMENT though not in the PSALM
My last's in HOSANNA but not in the PALM

 My whole is where Jesus went to school

D. My first's not in DESERT though where there is GRASS
My next's not in FIRST TIME but always in LAST
My third is in LANDING and also in LAKE
My fourth's not in ERROR but in a MISTAKE
My next helps in LIFE and in LOVE and in LIGHT
My sixth's twice in LEFT SIDE but never in RIGHT
My last comes full three times in ENDLESS DELIGHT

 My whole is a New Testament region and sea

45. NAAMAN VISITS THE PROPHET

ALL answers appear in 2 Kings 5:1–19.

1. Elisha's kind words to Naaman: "Go in . . ."
2. King of Israel tore his
3. Naaman should do this in the Jordan
4. How Naaman left Elisha's messenger
5. Elisha's servant
6. Naaman's illness
7. The man of God
8. Naaman's nationality
9. Israel's river
10. What Naaman did at Elisha's door
11. Naaman became this when he washed in the Jordan
12. A young one served Naaman's wife

Center column: Two rivers of Damascus

46. BIBLE LANDS AND PROVINCES

THE words appear forward, backward, upward, downward, and diagonally.

```
A M O S A M A R I A H O
I E P Y A E A W B C X C
C D B L T S D M A R A T
Y I T R U O T F I E D L
L A X R N P O N T U S M
Q G P I Y O H L A K Y P
H Y A G P T Y R L M R E
C P E M U A C A Y P I R
S B E D O M H M I G A S
O D I E U I S S A D I I
C J U D E A U C P L N A
L N A A N A C R E T E O
```

ARAM	EDOM	LYCIA	PHRYGIA
CANAAN	ELAM	MALTA	PONTUS
COS	EGYPT	MEDIA	SAMARIA
CRETE	ITALY	MESOPOTAMIA	SPAIN
CUSH	JUDEA	NOD	SYRIA
CYPRUS	LIBYA	PERSIA	

47. TEN TENTS

EACH answer contains the letters TENT. Supply the missing word in each line.

1. "They speak of you with evil _____" (Ps. 139:20)
2. "Godliness with _____ is great gain" (1 Tim. 6:6)
3. After-school punishment is _____
4. "We must pay more careful _____, therefore, to what we have heard" (Heb. 2:1)
5. "All your _____ spells" (Isa. 47:9)
6. "To some _____ I believe it" (1 Cor. 11:18)
7. "_____ to instruct one another" (Rom. 15:14)
8. A thief at Calvary was a _____
9. Portion to be given to God of mint and garden herbs was a _____ (Matt. 23:23)
10. "I have become like a _____ to many" (Ps. 71:7)

48. SIX-LETTER NAMES

ADD the first three letters to each name.

1. _____ RAH   Where an angel sat under an oak tree (Judg. 6:11)
2. _____ RAH   Amos prophesied its destruction (Amos 1:12)
3. _____ RAM   Son of Eliab (Num. 16:1)
4. _____ RAT   Mountain of the ark's resting-place (Gen. 8:4)
5. _____ REW   Peter's brother (Matt. 4:18)
6. _____ REW   Paul, by race
7. _____ ROD   Mighty hunter (Gen. 10:9)
8. _____ RON   Valley in Jerusalem
9. _____ RON   He sold Machpelah to Abraham (Gen. 23:17)
10. _____ RON   City of refuge (Josh. 20:7)
11. _____ RUS   Mediterranean island (Acts 11:19)
12. _____ RUS   Synagogue ruler (Mark 5:22)

49. LINKING UP

A. Join these groups of letters in twos or threes and make twelve
New Testament books.

MATT   JO   ES   MA   TI   ANS

LU   MOTH   DE   TION

REV   RK   HN   PHI   JU   Y

PE   LEMON   TUS   TER   KE

COLO   ELA   SSI   HEW   JAM   TI

B. Join these groups of letters in pairs to name ten altar-builders.

NO   SA   JA   ON

ISA   GIDE   AH   AB

VID   COB   MUEL   JOS   AM

RAM   BALA   DA   AC   ES

HUA   MOS

50. ALL IN THE FAMILY

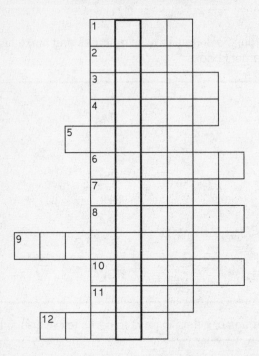

ALL center column letters are the same.

1. Cousin of Barnabas (Col. 4:10)
2. Mother of John Mark (Acts 12:12)
3. Brother of Miriam (Exod. 15:20)
4. Grandson of Obed (Matt. 1:5–6)
5. Grandfather of Judah (Matt. 1:2)
6. Sister of Mary (Luke 10:38–39)
7. Mother-in-law of Ruth (Ruth 1:4–5)
8. Father of Noah (Gen. 5:28)
9. Son of Rachel (Gen. 35:18)
10. Grandmother of Ephraim (Gen. 48:7)
11. Nephew of Ner (1 Sam. 14:50)
12. Daughter of Leah (Gen. 30:21)

51. ALL IN THE WARDROBE

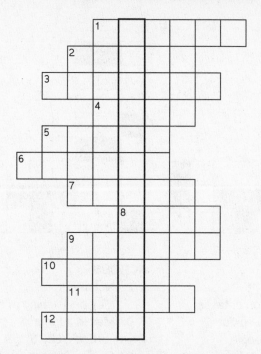

1. Worn by Shadrach and his friends (Dan. 3:21)
2. Pharaoh dressed Joseph in fine . . . (Gen. 41:42)
3. To be taken off on holy ground (Exod. 3:5)
4. Face covering (Exod. 34:33)
5. Worn as part of finery (Isa. 3:23)
6. Jacob ordered his household: ". . . your clothes" (Gen. 35:2)
7. Ruth's was filled with barley (Ruth 3:15)
8. Best one was put on the prodigal son (Luke 15:22)
9. John the Baptist's clothing was made from this hair (Matt. 3:4)
10. Worn in Isaiah's time with fine robes and cloaks (Isa. 3:22)
11. Twelve disciples could not take an extra one (Luke 9:3)
12. Agabus took this from Paul (Acts 21:11)

Center column: Worn beneath all others

52. THREES AND SEVENS

A.

B.

ACROSS

2. A testament
5. . . . attention or taxes
6. Made by a spider
9. Race of people
13. Self-esteem
14. African antelope
15. Son of Noah (Gen. 5:32)

DOWN

1. God told Moses to "go to the . . . of Pisgah" (Deut 3:27)
3. Given by Moses
4. Stain
7. . . . nabas
8. Not he
10. Goes with bacon
11. Good in France
12. Ocean

ACROSS

2. Not dry
5. May be listening or deaf
6. Melt in a furnace (Ezek. 22:18)
9. Old Testament prophet
13. Not one left in the wall by Nehemiah
14. Used by a fisherman
15. Mineral spring

DOWN

1. To be in debt
3. Devour
4. Prefix for three
7. Cain lived here (Gen. 4:16)
8. Thick mist
10. Not allow
11. Monkey
12. Body joint

53. THE SHEPHERD'S PSALM

TWO words are filled in to help you. All words can be found in Psalm 23.

IN	HEAD	PATHS	PASTURES
CUP	LORD	BESIDE	PRESENCE
OIL	LOVE	GUIDES	SHEPHERD
ROD	DWELL	SHADOW	RIGHTEOUSNESS
THE	DEATH	SURELY	
DAYS	HOUSE	PREPARE	

54. BIBLE ALTARS

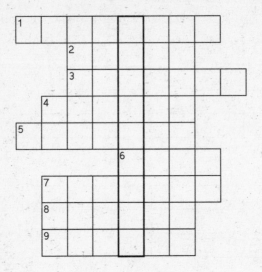

1. Where Ahaz saw an altar (2 Kings 16:10)
2. Who was Abraham going to offer on an altar? (Gen. 22:9)
3. They burned this on altars of brick (Isa. 65:3)
4. Where Gideon built an altar (Judg. 6:24)
5. Asa removed these altars (2 Chron. 14:3)
6. It burned up Elijah's sacrifice (1 Kings 18:38)
7. With the Reubenites they built an altar called "A Witness Between Us that the LORD is God" (Josh. 22:34)
8. Moses built an altar of . . . wood (Exod. 27:1)
9. Where Paul found an altar to an unknown god (Acts 17:22–23)

Center column: Offered on an altar

55. MUDDLED VERSES

IN each case find the verse in the given chapter and write the correct words on a piece of paper.

1. The way I am and the life and the truth (John 14)
2. I am the gardener and my Father is the true vine (John 15)
3. He binds up the broken-hearted and he heals their wounds (Ps. 147)
4. You will find me and seek me when you find me with all your heart (Jer. 29)
5. Love yourself as your neighbor (Rom. 13)
6. Lift up yourselves, therefore, under God's mighty hand, that he may humble you in due time (1 Peter 5)
7. Love must be sincere. Cling to what is evil; hate what is good (Rom. 12)
8. Store up for yourselves moth and rust in heaven, where treasures do not destroy (Matt. 6)
9. As I will be with Moses, so I was with you (Josh. 1)
10. You will keep steadfast him whose mind is in perfect peace (Isa. 26)
11. Live in harmony . . . as brothers; be sympathetic, love one another (1 Peter 3)
12. Love does not delight with the truth but rejoices in evil (1 Cor. 13)

56. COLLECTIVE NOUNS

ADD the missing words and verse numbers.

1. Band of _____ 1 Kings 11: _____

2. Brood of _____ Matthew 3: _____

3. Bunch of _____ Exodus 12: _____

4. Cluster of _____ Numbers 13: _____

5. Droves of _____ Exodus 12: _____

6. Detachment of _____ John 18: _____

7. Flock of _____ Matthew 26: _____

8. Heap of _____ Jeremiah 51: _____

9. Herd of _____ Mark 5: _____

10. Host of _____ Luke 2: _____

11. Pile of _____ Ezra 6: _____

12. Swarm of _____ Jeremiah 51: _____

57. SQUARES OF NINE

LOOK for a starting letter in each small square; then build up a word or name, moving to an adjacent letter each time, horizontally, vertically, or diagonally.

A.

1	2	3

```
  1         2         3
 E U S    Y O M    M U S
 A A C    N T I    E N I
 H C Z    E S T    D O C

 S R A    S L P    B B E
4A M I    E S I    E U Z 5
 N A T    D I C    B E L

 E M E    H Z P    H P S
 N N A    A E H    E E N
 T T O    I N A    S I A
  6         7         8
```

B.

```
  9        10        11
 H T E    T A L    P I E
 L B E    I A V    T A N
 E H M    S O N    S E L

 S E C    O P S    A A I
12I A D    T L I    M C N 13
 L O P    E M A    E D O

 R U J    R E P    I L Y
 S E E    N A C    U L R
 A L M    A U M    M C I
  14        15        16
```

1. Tax collector (Luke 19:2)
2. Witness
3. Night visitor (John 3:1–2)
4. Kind traveler (Luke 10:33)
5. Prince of demons (Matt. 12:24)
6. Made at Calvary
7. Prophet
8. Epistle

Center: Followers of Jesus

9. Birthplace of Jesus (Matt. 2:1)
10. Seen by Simeon's eyes (Luke 2:30)
11. Earlier name of Israel
12. District of ten Greek cities (Matt. 4:25)
13. Visited by Paul after a night vision (Acts 16:9)
14. Capital of Judah
15. Where Jesus healed Peter's mother-in-law (Mark 1:21, 30–31)
16. Paul preached the gospel from "Jerusalem all the way around to . . ." (Rom. 15:19)

Center: Visited by Paul before he went to Caesarea (Acts 21:7)

58. MEN AND WOMEN

OF THE BIBLE

A. Men

B. Women

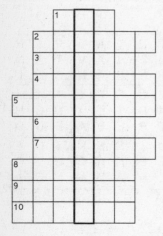

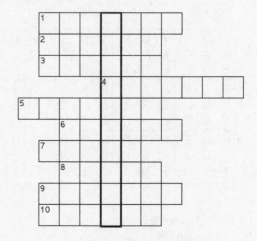

1. Son of Noah (Gen. 9:18)
2. Man of the vineyard
   (1 Kings 21:1)
3. Had a well in Sychar (John 4:5)
4. Brought his brother Simon to
   Jesus (John 1:41)
5. A son of Moses (1 Chron. 23:15)
6. His father carried the cross for
   Jesus (Mark 15:21)
7. Prophet in the days of King
   Darius (Ezra 5:1)
8. Told the parable of the ewe
   lamb (2 Sam. 12:1–3)
9. Prophet, son of Amoz (Isa. 1:1)
10. Successor to Rehoboam
    (1 Kings 14:31)

1. Nabal's wife (1 Sam. 25:3)
2. Queen instead of Vashti
   (Esther 2:17)
3. Played a tambourine
   (Exod. 15:20)
4. Eaten by dogs (2 Kings 9:36)
5. Mother of Jacob (Gen. 25:26)
6. Mother of Tubal-Cain
   (Gen. 4:22)
7. Wife of Elimelech (Ruth 1:2)
8. Leah's daughter (Gen. 30:21)
9. Rebekah's nurse (Gen. 35:8)
10. Lydia sold this cloth
    (Acts 16:14)

Center column: Letters in alphabetical order

Center column: Letters in
alphabetical order

59. WHEELS OF KNOWLEDGE

FILL in the spaces according to the clues. The last letter or letters of answer no. 1 are the same as the first letter or letters of answer no. 2, and so on. Each new word starts a new circle.

A.

1. Its walls fell down (Josh. 6:2)
2. Old Testament book
3. Seven in the Revelation (5:1)
4. Jewish priest with seven sons (Acts 19:14)
5. A testimony must be
6. False god
7. Jerusalem mountain (Matt. 21:1)

B.

1. Paul arrived here after leaving Rhegium (Acts 28:13)
2. David said they had fallen for him in pleasant places (Ps. 16:6)
3. Homes of birds
4. Imprisoned with Paul in Philippi (Acts 16:22)
5. Associated with repentance and sackcloth (Matt. 11:21)
6. Twin brother of Jacob (Gen. 25:26)
7. Time of rain according to Joel (2:23)

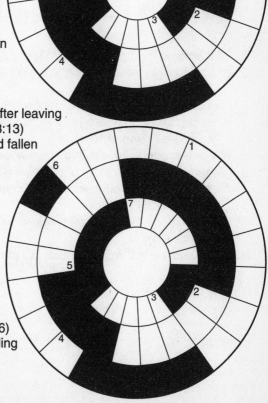

60. BY THE WINDOW

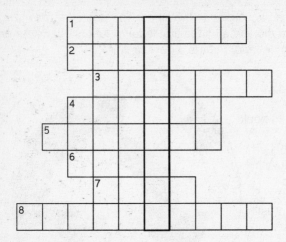

1. Who entered through windows? (Joel 2:9)
2. What king saw Jezebel sitting at a window in Jezreel? (2 Kings 9:31)
3. He looked through this at the window (Prov. 7:6)
4. What did Daniel do where the windows opened towards Jerusalem? (Dan. 6:10)
5. Where a scarlet cord was tied in a window (Josh. 2:3)
6. He opened a window to let out a raven (Gen. 8:6–7)
7. Who was lowered from a window in Damascus? (Acts 9:24–25)
8. Solomon made these narrow windows in the temple (1 Kings 6:4)

Center column: He fell from a window in Troas (Acts 20:9)

61. TWENTY BROKEN VERSES

FILL in the missing words and the answers will come in alphabetical order.

1. Break down their _____ (Exod. 34:13)
2. Jesus took _____, gave thanks and broke it (Matt. 26:26)
3. The people have broken my _____ (Hos. 8:1)
4. Starting a quarrel is like breaching a _____ (Prov. 17:14)
5. The _____ is broken up (Isa. 24:19)
6. How could you break _____ with the God of Israel like this? (Josh. 22:16)
7. I will break down _____ of bronze (Isa. 45:2)
8. A broken and contrite _____, O God, you will not despise (Ps. 51:17)
9. Can a man break _____ from the north—or bronze? (Jer. 15:12)
10. She broke the _____ and poured the perfume on his head (Mark 14:3)
11. It is time for you to act, O LORD, your _____ is being broken (Ps. 119:126)
12. You will break to pieces many _____ (Mic. 4:13)
13. Do not break your _____ you have made to the Lord (Matt. 5:33)
14. I have become like broken _____ (Ps. 31:12)
15. The LORD has broken the _____ of the wicked (Isa. 14:5)
16. The _____ cannot be broken (John 10:35)
17. I will write on them the words that were on the first _____, which you broke (Exod. 34:1)
18. Break up your _____ ground (Jer. 4:3)
19. The _____ of Jerusalem is broken down (Neh. 1:3)
20. I will break the _____ off their necks (Jer. 30:8)

62. CATCHING FISH

1. Time of Simon's fishing
   (Luke 5:5)
2. Fishing tackle (Amos 4:2)
3. Thrown into the lake by
   Peter (Matt. 17:27)
4. (Across) Wrote about fishing
   in 1 Kings 4:33
   (Down) Place for fishing
5. Another fishing place
6. Bible sea (John 6:1)
7. A fish caught him
8. Result of fishing
9. Put out into . . . water
   (Luke 5:4)
10. Brother of fisherman Peter
    (Luke 6:14)

11. Natural habitat of fish
12. Galilean fisherman
    (Matt. 4:21)
13. Fishing mesh
14. Fishing pole (Job 41:7)
15. Found in a fish's mouth
16. Land of fishermen
17. Fisherman who jumped into
    the water (John 21:7)
18. I will make you fishers of . . .
19. Sailing vessel for fishermen
20. Where fish died (Exod. 7:18)
21. After the resurrection Jesus
    took a piece of . . . fish
    (Luke 24:42)

63. CHANGING LETTERS

CHANGE one letter at a time to find a connected word.

A. M   O   R   E

— — — — Apple center
— — — — ". . . to me, all who are weary"
— — — — Cathedral top
— — — — Coin
— — — — "Jesus asked him the third . . ." (John 21:17)
— — — — Fruit
— — — — Hands can hang this way (Jer. 6:24)
— — — — Imperfect speech
— — — — Roster
— — — — . . . we forget
— — — — A minus sign

B. G   I   V   E

— — — — You . . . me something to drink
— — — — Talk wildly
— — — — Speed
— — — — A male animal entered the ark with its . . .
— — — — Widow's gift
— — — — Could be deaf as well
— — — — Played with a tambourine and harp
— — — — Third Gospel
— — — — Similar
— — — — Sea or . . . of Galilee
— — — — Opposite of give

C. H   O   P   E

— — — — Nazareth was . . . to Jesus
— — — — End of Paul's travels
— — — — Rahab let them down by a . . . (Josh. 2:15)
— — — — Head of the Roman Catholic Church
— — — — Done for a photographer
— — — — "Every night I [the lookout] stay at my . . ." (Isa. 21:8)
— — — — Price
— — — — Son, coin, and sheep in Luke 15
— — — — Misplace
— — — — Part of the ear
— — — — Greater than hope (1 Cor. 13)

64. BIBLE WORKERS AND MATERIALS

TWO words are printed in from the list below to start you off.

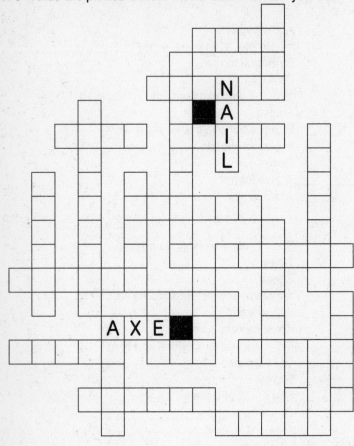

NET	WOOD	STONE	WRITER
PEN	ANVIL	ARTIST	BUILDER
BOAT	BAKER	FISHER	GOLDSMITH
CLAY	BRICK	POTTER	CARPENTER
DYER	MASON	SILVER	
IRON	PAINT	TAILOR	
PLOW	PAPER	TANNER	

65. COLUMNS OF TRUTH

START the missing word in the square provided, as in the given example.

A.

1. Easter message—"He is . . ."
2. Jacob and . . .
3. Paul's conversion on the road to . . . (Acts 9:3)
4. "Your word, O LORD, is . . ." (Ps. 119:89)
5. Noon is also . . .
6. . . . and Silas
7. . . . commandments
8. Jeroboam, king of . . .
9. Mount of . . . (Matt. 21:1)
10. . . . was a mighty hunter (Gen. 10:9)

R	isen

Column: Appears twice in Ephesians 1

B.

1. Heaven and . . .
2. The same . . . and today and forever (Heb. 13:8)
3. . . . lamb
4. . . . of Bashan (Isa. 2:13)
5. To . . . favor (Prov. 19:6)
6. . . . and a purifier of silver (Mal. 3:3)
7. Judas . . .
8. . . . offering
9. . . . doer
10. man . . .

Column: How Jesus described some inquiring Pharisees (Matt. 15:7)

66. TIME OF ELIJAH AND ELISHA

A. Rearrange each set of letters and discover a king's name.

1. N IS HIM   _____ Jehu's father
   (2 Kings 9:2)

2. OR JAM   _____ He got rid of the
   sacred stone of
   Baal (2 Kings 3:1–2)

3. A H LAZE   _____ Anointed by Elijah
   (1 Kings 19:15)

4. HE OR JAM   _____ Father of Jehosheba
   (2 Kings 11:2)

5. O HE HATH JAPS_____ He built a fleet of trading
   ships (1 Kings 22:48)

6. HUJE   _____ He drove like a madman
   (2 Kings 9:20)

7. A BED HAND   _____ A king of Aram
   (1 Kings 20:1)

8. HA HA AZI   _____ He fell from an upper
   room (2 Kings 1:2)

B. Rearrange each set of letters and discover a place name.

1. HIS BET   _____ Home of Elijah
   (1 Kings 17:1)

2. I AS A RAM   _____ Capital of Israel

3. RECLAM   _____ Mountain of Baal's defeat
   (1 Kings 18:19)

4. RAZE H PATH   _____ Home of a widow
   (1 Kings 17:9)

5. GLADIATOR HEM_____ Elisha went there with a
   flask of oil (2 Kings 9:1)

6. HER KIT   _____ Where Elijah was fed by
   ravens (1 Kings 17:3)

7. A SAD SCUM   _____ City of Syria

8. SUM HEN   _____ Where Elijah restored
   a boy to life

67. CRISS-CROSS

THE words appear forward, backward, upward, downward, or diagonally. Circle each word. All words are from the Bible.

A. Traveling Along

```
C  K  H  O  R  S  E
H  L  D  T  R  A  C
A  M  R  O  A  D  A
R  E  I  N  S  D  M
I  L  V  L  P  L  E
O  X  E  A  E  E  L
T  A  R  N  E  U  W
P  Q  R  E  D  I  R
```

AXLE	CAMEL	CART	CHARIOT	DRIVER
HORSE	LANE	MILE	REINS	RIDER
ROAD	SADDLE	SPEED		

B. In the Garden

```
A  R  P  K  M  K  D
Z  I  L  N  V  R  D
C  D  A  I  O  O  N
F  E  N  O  O  F  U
R  E  T  B  D  S  O
U  W  R  E  R  I  R
I  O  E  Q  P  E  G
T  S  E  V  R  A  H
```

DIG	FORK	FRUIT	GROUND	HARVEST
HERB	PLANT	ROOT	SEED	SOIL
SOW	TREE	VINE	WEED	

68. MORE SIX-LETTER NAMES

ADD the first three letters of each name.

1. _____ AEL Anointed King of Aram by Elijah
2. _____ BUS A prophet of Jerusalem
3. _____ CAS Robe-maker also called Tabitha
4. _____ DOD City of the Philistines where they worshiped Dagon
5. _____ EON He beat the Midianites with 300 men
6. _____ GAL Where the Israelites erected a twelve-stone memorial
7. _____ HER Queen of Xerxes
8. _____ ILA Priscilla's husband
9. _____ JAH Prophet who wore a hair coat and leather belt
10. _____ LEK Grandson of Esau
11. _____ MON Mountain
12. _____ NAH Mother of Samuel
13. _____ OAM Pool in Jerusalem
14. _____ PUS Paul left his cloak with him
15. _____ RAM Descendant of Benjamin
16. _____ SIA Now called Iran
17. _____ TUS Successor to Felix
18. _____ UCH Jeremiah's scribe

69. GOING TO MARKET

THE words appear forward, backward, upward, downward, or diagonally. Circle each word. All the words are from the Bible.

```
P L E N T I L C P H D F
O I Z U F L O U R A L G
M U S T A R D R D Y R I
E I N T N H Y R J A I F
G O L O A M U A P P L E
R Y A K M C D E E S O V
A E E S E E H C Q L N I
N C T N P E L I A R O L
A O K T O E L P O L I O
T W L Y U H L S W I N E
E N A E B B D T T A O G
C D N O M L A M B B M G
```

ALMOND	ALOE	APPLE	BEAN
BUTTER	CHEESE	CORN	COW
CURD	FIG	FLOUR	GOAT
GRAPE	HAY	HONEY	LAMB
LEEK	LEMON	LENTIL	MELON
MILK	MUSTARD	MYRRH	NUT
OIL	OLIVE	ONION	PISTACHIO
POMEGRANATE	SEED	SPELT	SPICE
WINE			

70. ON THE SEA IN SHIPS

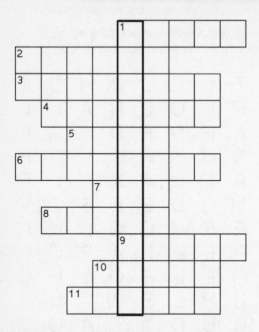

1. Where Jonah found a ship (Jonah 1:3)
2. By what small thing is a large ship steered? (James 3:4)
3. A good wife is like this sort of ship (Prov. 31:14)
4. Who built ships at Ezion Geber? (1 Kings 9:26)
5. What people will be frightened by messengers in ships? (Ezek. 30:9)
6. Ships from here were shattered by an east wind (Ps. 48:7)
7. Who lingered by the ships? (Judg. 5:17)
8. Where would the Lord send the disobedient in ships? (Deut. 28:68)
9. He brought gold in ships (1 Kings 10:11)
10. Paul was shipwrecked near this island (Acts 28:1)
11. Where did Paul find a ship for Phoenicia? (Acts 21:1–2)

Center column: Who had a fleet of sailing ships which never set sail? (1 Kings 22:48)

71. BIBLE SINGING

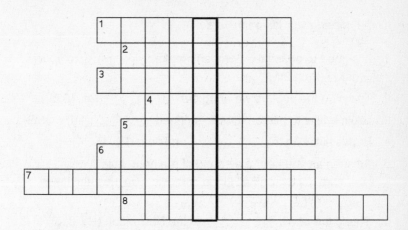

1. Paul and Silas sang hymns in the prison of this city (Acts 16)
2. "I will sing . . . to your name" (Ps. 18:49)
3. The Ephesians should sing these songs (Eph. 5:19)
4. In Tyre there will be "an end to your . . . songs" (Ezek. 26:13)
5. God's people burst into this song (Ps. 98:4)
6. When God rejected Israel there were no . . . songs (Ps. 78:63)
7. Jonah's song was one of . . . (Jonah 2:9)
8. David was surrounded by songs of . . . (Ps. 32:7)

You will see that the center column has a certain unity.

72. LOST STRINGS AND SOUNDS OF MUSIC

ADD the missing word in each verse.

1. It is good to praise the LORD and make _____ to your name (Ps. 92:1)

2. There on the poplars we hung our _____ (Ps. 137:2)

3. Make music to him on the ten-stringed _____ (Ps. 33:2)

4. Praise him with the _____ and flute (Ps. 150:4)

5. As soon as you hear the sound of the horn, flute, _____, lyre, harp, pipes, and all kinds of music, you must fall down and worship (Dan. 3:5)

6. Sound the ram's _____ at the New Moon (Ps. 81:3)

7. If the _____ does not sound a clear call, who will get ready for battle? (1 Cor. 14:8)

8. Miriam the prophetess, Aaron's sister, took a _____ in her hand (Exod. 15:20)

73. MISSING WORDS

FILL in the missing words and you will find that each answer describes a movement.

1. Those that have jointed legs for _____ on the ground (Lev. 11:21)

2. He _____ to his feet and came to Jesus (Mark 10:50)

3. Whoever follows me will never _____ in darkness (John 8:12)

4. Rejoice in that day and _____ for joy (Luke 6:23)

5. They will _____ and not grow weary (Isa. 40:31)

6. He ordered those who could _____ to jump overboard (Acts 27:43)

7. They lick dust like a snake, like creatures that _____ on the ground (Mic. 7:17)

8. Anyone who does not carry his cross and _____ me cannot be my disciple (Luke 14:27)

9. Let the water teem with living creatures, and let birds _____ above the earth (Gen. 1:20)

10. If a blind man leads a blind man, both will _____ into a pit (Matt. 15:14)

11. In your majesty _____ forth victoriously on behalf of truth (Ps. 45:4)

12. Resist the devil, and he will _____ from you (James 4:7)

74. ELIJAH ON CARMEL

ALL answers are found in 1 Kings 18:16–46.

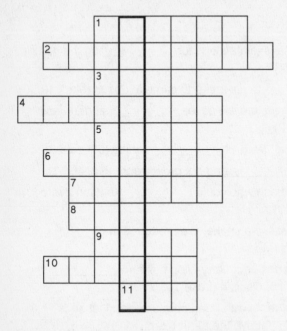

1. The prophets of Baal slashed themselves with these
2. Offered on Mount Carmel
3. When Elijah's taunts began
4. "Maybe he [Baal] is . . ."
5. King of Israel in Elijah's time
6. She had four hundred false prophets
7. Valley of slaughter
8. It grew black
9. It burned Elijah's sacrifice
10. With them Elijah built an altar
11. On Mount Carmel he was proved to be the one and only

Center column: The prophets of Baal were frantic in this action.

75. TEN LOTS

EACH answer contains the letters LOT.

1. Only one lot for the
   people of Joseph
   (Josh. 17:14) _____

2. A lot for district governor
   Baana (1 Kings 4:16) _____

3. A lot for dressmakers _____

4. This lot had a sister
   Timna (1 Chron. 1:39) _____

5. A lot of ointment _____

6. The behemoth lies under
   this lot (Job 40:21) _____

7. This lot was a divisional
   leader (1 Chron. 27:4) _____

8. A lot steering a ship _____

9. A lot for a schemer _____

10. A keen lot this
    (Matt. 10:4) _____

ANSWERS

1. Bible Dreams

1. Pharaoh	3. Magi	5. Joseph	7. Cares	9. Night
2. Laban	4. Solomon	6. Pilate	8. Jacob	

Center column: Abimelech

2. Regroup the Letters

1. Psalm 8:9
2. John 6:37
3. 1 Thessalonians 5:13
4. Psalm 7:10
5. 1 Timothy 6:6
6. Psalm 29:11
7. 1 Peter 5:7

3. Same for Three

1. Hand	3. Off	5. Free	7. Cross	9. High
2. Foot	4. God	6. Man	8. Door/Gate	10. Ever

4. Eight Bible Gates

1. Adullam	3. Crippled	5. Elders	7. Guard
2. Boaz	4. Damascus	6. Flood	8. Horse

5. In All Directions

A.

B.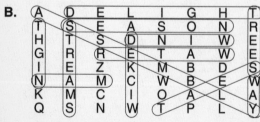

C.

D.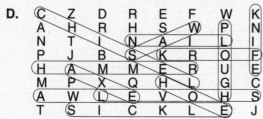

6. Who Are We?

A. Philemon   **B.** Matthias   **C.** Thyatira   **D.** Benjamin

7. Let's Go to Work

1. Embalmers 3. Weaver 5. Baker   7. Tentmaker 9. Potter
2. Fuller   4. Bricks   6. Masons 8. Spindle   10. Matthew

Center column: Blacksmith

8. Ten Full Urns

1. Burnt   3. Furnace   5. Laburnum   7. Nocturnal 9. Spurn
2. Churning 4. Journey 6. Mourn   8. Return   10. Turn

9. Jumbled Countries

1. Persia   4. Phrygia   7. Ethiopia   10. Cappadocia
2. Cyprus   5. Pamphylia   8. Assyria
3. Egypt   6. Macedonia   9. Crete

10. Sailing Away

1. Boat   3. Oars   5. Mast   7. Kittim   9. Pilot   11. Solomon
2. Deck   4. Jonah 6. Tyre   8. Storm   10. Rudder

Center column: Adramyttium

11. Lost Words

"Look, the Lamb of God, who takes away the sin of the world" (John 1:29).

12. Pyramids

A.

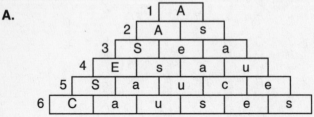

1	A				
2	A	s			
3	S	e	a		
4	E	s	a	u	
5	S	a	u	c	e
6	C	a	u	s	e	s

B.

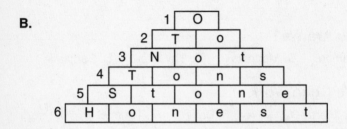

1	O				
2	T	o			
3	N	o	t		
4	T	o	n	s	
5	S	t	o	n	e
6	H	o	n	e	s	t

13. Limericks

A. Nain, Cheer
B. Jesus, Beatitudes
C. Barnabas, Lystra
D. Athens, Altar

14. Changing Letters

A.	MORN	**B.**	CAIN	**C.**	HOLD
	MOAN		COIN		HELD
	LOAN		LOIN		HEAD
	LOAF		LOIS		HEAT
			LOSS		

15. Regroup More Letters

1. Ephesians 5:2   3. Galatians 6:10   5. Matthew 6:33   7. Psalm 27:1
2. Psalm 28:7   4. Job 5:17   6. James 5:16

16. Names and Places

Adam	Gideon	Mysia	Rebekah	Widow
Babel	Herod	Noah	Samaritan	Xerxes
Canaan	Isaiah	Ophir	Timothy	Yellow
Decapolis	Japheth	Peter	Uriah	Zebedee
Egypt	Kish	Quails	Vineyard	
Felix	Lazarus			

17. A Bible Wardrobe

1. Dress
2. Camel
3. Robes
4. Charms
5. Wool
6. Tiaras
7. Sandals
8. Capes
9. Purple
10. Linen
11. Body

Center column: Embroidered

18. Add the Figures

1. 12
2. 1
3. 40
4. 2
5. 3
6. 8
7. 5
8. 6
9. 9
10. 30
11. 4
12. 10

19. In the Desert

1. Highway
2. Quail
3. Calf
4. Judea
5. Kadesh
6. Korah
7. Manna
8. Red
9. Moses
10. Passover

Center column: Wilderness

20. Mini-Crosswords

A. Across
1. Hit
3. Man
5. Ate
7. Art
9. End
10. All
11. Din

Down
1. Ham
2. Ten
4. Ant
5. Ada
6. Eel
7. Add
8. Tin

B. Across
1. Tan
3. Rod
5. Ben
7. Saw
9. Oak
10. War
11. Yen

Down
1. Tar
2. Nod
4. One
5. Bow
6. Nor
7. Sky
8. Win

21. Strip Words

A. Lebanon
B. Syracuse
C. Capernaum
D. Samothrace
E. Mesopotamia
F. Philadelphia

22. Wells and Springs

1. Beersheba 3. Bethlehem 5. Parched 7. Sirah 9. Princes
2. Baca 4. Ravines 6. Righteous 8. Jacob

Center column: Salvation

23. Things in Common

A.
1. Seas
2. Kings of Israel
3. Towns in Galilee
4. Parables of Jesus
5. Apostles of Jesus
6. Sons of Jacob
7. Spiritual gifts
8. Parts of a church
9. New Testament books
10. Hometown was Bethsaida

B.
1. Sons of Noah
2. Wise men's gifts to Jesus
3. Churches in the Revelation
4. Old Testament characters
5. Kings of Judah
6. Prophets
7. Rivers flowing from Eden
8. Musical instruments
9. Mountains
10. Lights in the sky

24. Psalm Forty-Six

25. Make the Trio

1. Ham
2. Myrrh
3. Noon

4. Father
5. Greek
6. Shadrach

7. Water
8. Eat
9. Love

10. Truth
11. Mene

26. Hidden Bible Rivers

1. Abana
2. Jordan

3. Habor
4. Kebar

5. Pishon
6. Pharpar

7. Arnon
8. Gihon

27. The First Psalm

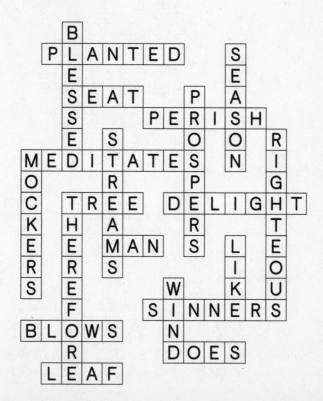

28. The Hundredth Psalm

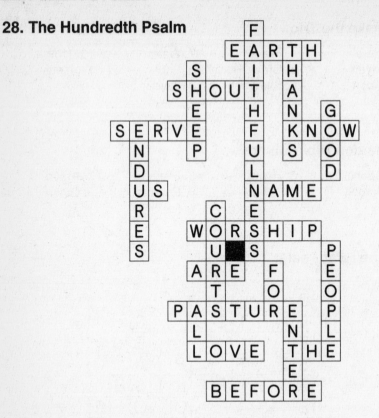

29. Help in Time of Need

1. Afraid	3. Inlaid	5. Maid	7. Paid	9. Said
2. Braid	4. Laid	6. Mislaid	8. Raid	10. Staid

30. Bible Places

1. Israel	6. Hebron	11. Emmaus	16. Sardis
2. Cyprus	7. Lystra	12. Paphos	17. Bashan
3. Ashdod	8. Rhodes	13. Arabia	18. Gilboa
4. Carmel	9. Pisgah	14. Smyrna	19. Cyrene
5. Jordan	10. Sychar	15. Ziklag	20. Gilead

31. Bible People

1. Samuel	6. Esther	11. Samson	16. Reuben
2. Thomas	7. Joshua	12. Philip	17. Xerxes
3. Joseph	8. Lamech	13. Shemer	18. Baasha
4. Abijam	9. Aquila	14. Hanani	19. Bildad
5. Haggai	10. Eunice	15. Darius	20. Pilate

32. The Traders Are Coming

1. Shekels	4. Tarshish	7. Gold
2. Purple	5. Caravans	8. Chariot
3. Scales	6. Lebanon	9. Horses

Center column: Merchandise

33. Outspoken Prophets

1. Elijah	6. Ahijah	11. Elisha
2. Ezekiel	7. Agabus	12. Joel
3. Aaron	8. Nahum	13. Hosea
4. Oded	9. Shemaiah	
5. Samuel	10. Noah	

Center column: (a) Jeremiah; (b) Moses

34. Seven-Letter Words

A.	**B.**	**C.**
1. Matthew	1. Grumble	1. Apollos
2. Weather	2. Ephesus	2. Samaria
3. Royalty	3. Solomon	3. Antioch
4. Yielded	4. Nothing	4. Heathen
5. Deliver	5. Galilee	5. Nineveh
6. Revenge	6. Emperor	6. Harvest
7. Eliakim	7. Reaping	7. Talitha

35. Metals and Minerals

1. Salt	4. Clay	7. Tin	10. Copper
2. Sand	5. Lead	8. Gold	11. Bronze
3. Soda	6. Silver	9. Iron	

Center column: A's, I's, O's

36. Crossword

ACROSS

1. Solomon	7. Oversee	11. Message	17. Nun
6. Eat	8. Sisters	15. Isobars	18. Teenage

DOWN

1. Scots	4. Mtsae (Meats)	10. Rag	13. Abana
2. Leeks	5. Needs	11. Moist	14. Elsie
3. Oar	9. Ice	12. Stone	16. Bun

37. Parents and Children

1. Adam	6. Saul	11. Noah
2. Ahaz	7. Caleb	12. Isaiah
3. Asher	8. Samuel	13. Maacah
4. Amaziah	9. David	
5. Jacob	10. Boaz	

38. Twos and Threes

A.

Italy	Silas	James	Crete
Jonah	Malta	Jacob	Egypt
Peter	Sidon	Laban	Derbe

B.

Judas	Herod	Jesse	Ophir
David	Asher	Joash	Samos
Titus	Chloe	Marah	Tubal

39. More Names and Places

Abigail	Gilboa	Lamech	Quartus	Vashti
Bethel	Hermon	Malachi	Romans	Winter
Crete	Isaac	Naboth	Shechem	Xerxes
Deborah	Joash	Og	Tarsus	Yaudi
Elisha	Kidron	Persia	Ur	Zalmon
Festus				

40. The Fourth Commandment

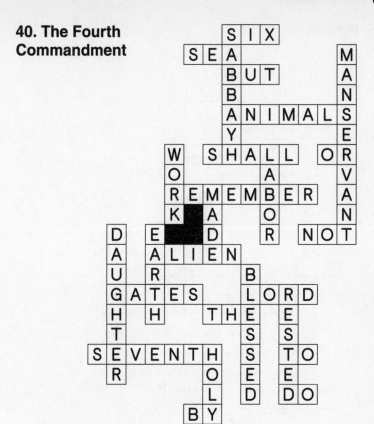

41. Threes and Fours

A. Samaria   Joseph   Dorcas   Ananias
    Athens   Calvary   Nazareth   Samuel
    Canaan   Sardis   Antioch   Sapphira
B. Cyprus   Lystra   Tarshish   Festus
    Jordan   Elijah   Hannah   Eunice
    Arabia   Salamis   Bethany   Gideon

42. More Pyramids
A.

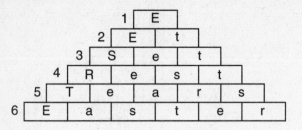

1	E				
2	E	t			
3	S	e	t		
4	R	e	s	t	
5	T	e	a	r	s
6	E	a	s	t	e	r

B.

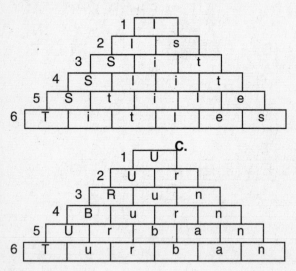

1	I				
2	I	s			
3	S	i	t		
4	S	l	i	t	
5	S	t	i	l	e
6	T	i	t	l	e	s

C.

1	U				
2	U	r			
3	R	u	n		
4	B	u	r	n	
5	U	r	b	a	n
6	T	u	r	b	a	n

43. Land of Egypt

1. Straw	4. Aswan	7. Pharaoh
2. Miriam	5. Moses	8. Joseph
3. Rameses	6. Locusts	9. Passover

Center column: Treasures

44. Who Are We Again?

A. Bethany **B.** Jericho **C.** Nazareth **D.** Galilee

45. Naaman Visits the Prophet

1. Peace	4. Angry	7. Elisha	10. Stopped
2. Robes	5. Gehazi	8. Aramean	11. Cleansed
3. Wash	6. Leprosy	9. Jordan	12. Girl

Center column: Abana, Pharpar

46. Bible Lands and Provinces

47. Ten Tents

1. Intent	4. Attention	7. Competent	10. Portent
2. Contentment	5. Potent	8. Penitent	
3. Detention	6. Extent	9. Tenth	

48. Six-Letter Names

1. Ophrah	4. Ararat	7. Nimrod	10. Hebron
2. Bozrah	5. Andrew	8. Kidron	11. Cyprus
3. Abiram	6. Hebrew	9. Ephron	12. Jairus

49. Linking Up

A.

Matthew	Mark	Luke	John
Revelation	Peter	Jude	Titus
Colossians	James	Philemon	Timothy

B.

Jacob	Moses	Gideon	David
Noah	Abram	Isaac	Balaam
Samuel	Joshua		

50. All in the Family

1. Mark	4. David	7. Naomi	10. Rachel
2. Mary	5. Isaac	8. Lamech	11. Saul
3. Aaron	6. Martha	9. Benjamin	12. Dinah

51. All in the Wardrobe

1. Turban	4. Veil	7. Shawl	10. Capes
2. Linen	5. Tiara	8. Robe	11. Tunic
3. Sandals	6. Change	9. Camels	12. Belt

Center column: Undergarment

52. Threes and Sevens

A. ACROSS	DOWN	B. ACROSS	DOWN
2. Old	1. Top	2. Wet	1. Owe
5. Pay	3. Law	5. Ear	3. Eat
6. Web	4. Dye	6. Tin	4. Tri
9. Hebrews	7. Bar	9. Obadiah	7. Nod
13. Ego	8. She	13. Gap	8. Fog
14. Gnu	10. Egg	14. Net	10. Ban
15. Ham	11. Bon	15. Spa	11. Ape
	12. Sea		12. Hip

53. The Shepherd's Psalm

54. Bible Altars

1. Damascus
2. Isaac
3. Incense
4. Ophrah
5. Foreign
6. Fire
7. Gadites
8. Acacia
9. Athens

Center column: Sacrifice

55. Muddled Verses

1. Verse 6
2. Verse 1
3. Verse 3
4. Verse 13
5. Verse 9
6. Verse 6
7. Verse 9
8. Verse 20
9. Verse 5
10. Verse 3
11. Verse 8
12. Verse 6

56. Collective Nouns

1. Rebels (v. 24)
2. Vipers (v. 7)
3. Hyssop (v. 22)
4. Grapes (v. 23)
5. Livestock (v. 38)
6. Soldiers (v. 3 or 12)
7. Sheep (v. 31)
8. Ruins (v. 37)
9. Pigs (v. 11)
10. Angels (vv.13–15)
11. Rubble (v. 11)
12. Locusts (v. 14)

57. Squares of Nine

A.
1. Zacchaeus
2. Testimony
3. Nicodemus
4. Samaritan
5. Beelzebub
6. Atonement
7. Zephaniah
8. Ephesians
Center: Disciples

B.
9. Bethlehem
10. Salvation
11. Palestine
12. Decapolis
13. Macedonia
14. Jerusalem
15. Capernaum
16. Illyricum
Center: Ptolemais

58. Men and Women of the Bible

A.
1. Ham
2. Naboth
3. Jacob
4. Andrew
5. Eliezer
6. Rufus
7. Haggai
8. Nathan
9. Isaiah
10. Abijah

B.
1. Abigail
2. Esther
3. Miriam
4. Jezebel
5. Rebekah
6. Zillah
7. Naomi
8. Dinah
9. Deborah
10. Purple

59. Wheels of Knowledge

A.
1. Jericho
2. Hosea
3. Seals
4. Sceva
5. Valid
6. Idol
7. Olives

B.
1. Puteoli
2. Lines
3. Nests
4. Silas
5. Ashes
6. Esau
7. Autumn

60. By the Window

1. Thieves
2. Jehu
3. Lattice
4. Prayed
5. Jericho
6. Noah
7. Saul
8. Clerestory
Center column: Eutychus

61. Twenty Broken Verses

1. Altars	6. Faith	11. Law	16. Scripture
2. Bread	7. Gates	12. Nations	17. Tablets
3. Covenant	8. Heart	13. Oath	18. Unplowed
4. Dam	9. Iron	14. Pottery	19. Wall
5. Earth	10. Jar	15. Rod	20. Yoke

62. Catching Fish

1. Night	6. Galilee	12. Zebedee	18. Men
2. Hook	7. Jonah	13. Net	19. Boat
3. Line	8. Catch	14. Spear	20. River
4. (Across) Solomon	9. Deep	15. Coin	21. Broiled
(Down) Sea	10. Andrew	16. Israel	
5. Lake	11. Water	17. Peter	

63. Changing Letters

A.	B.	C.
CORE	GAVE	HOME
COME	RAVE	ROME
DOME	RATE	ROPE
DIME	MATE	POPE
TIME	MITE	POSE
LIME	MUTE	POST
LIMP	LUTE	COST
LISP	LUKE	LOST
LIST	LIKE	LOSE
LEST	LAKE	LOBE
LESS	TAKE	LOVE

64. Bible Workers and Materials

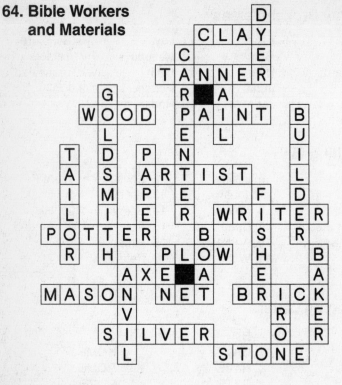

65. Columns of Truth

A.

1. Risen	3. Damascus	5. Midday	7. Ten	9. Olives
2. Esau	4. Eternal	6. Paul	8. Israel	10. Nimrod

Column: Redemption

B.

1. Hell	3. Passover	5. Curry	7. Iscariot	9. Evil
2. Yesterday	4. Oaks	6. Refiner	8. Thank	10. Servant

Column: Hypocrites

66. Time of Elijah and Elisha

A.

1. Nimshi	3. Hazael	5. Jehoshaphat	7. Ben Hadad
2. Joram	4. Jehoram	6. Jehu	8. Ahaziah

B.
  1. Tishbe   3. Carmel   5. Ramoth Gilead   7. Damascus
  2. Samaria 4. Zarephath 6. Kerith   8. Shunem

67. Criss-Cross

A. Traveling Along

B. In the Garden

68. More Six-Letter Names

1. Hazael	5. Gideon	9. Elijah	13. Siloam	17. Festus
2. Agabus	6. Gilgal	10. Amalek	14. Carpus	18. Baruch
3. Dorcas	7. Esther	11. Hermon	15. Ahiram	
4. Ashdod	8. Aquila	12. Hannah	16. Persia	

69. Going to Market

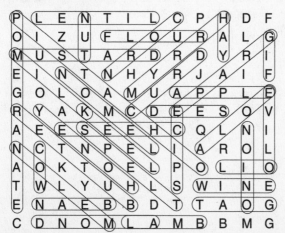

70. On the Sea in Ships

1. Joppa   4. Solomon   7. Dan   10. Malta
2. Rudder   5. Cush   8. Egypt   11. Patara
3. Merchant   6. Tarshish   9. Hiram

Center column: Jehoshaphat

71. Bible Singing

1. Philippi   3. Spiritual   5. Jubilant   7. Thanksgiving
2. Praises   4. Noisy   6. Wedding   8. Deliverance

72. Lost Strings and Sounds of Music

1. Music   3. Lyre   5. Zither   7. Trumpet
2. Harps   4. Strings   6. Horn   8. Tambourine

73. Missing Words

1. Hopping   4. Leap   7. Crawl   10. Fall
2. Jumped   5. Run   8. Follow   11. Ride
3. Walk   6. Swim   9. Fly   12. Flee

74. Elijah on Carmel

1. Spears   4. Sleeping   7. Kishon   10. Stones
2. Sacrifice   5. Ahab   8. Sky   11. God
3. Noon   6. Asherah   9. Fire

Center column: Prophesying

75. Ten Lots

1. Allotment   3. Cloth   5. Lotion   7. Mikloth   9. Plot
2. Aloth   4. Lotan   6. Lotus   8. Pilot   10. Zealot